SO
DONE

PAULA CHASE

SO
DONE

GREENWILLOW BOOKS

AN IMPRINT OF HarperCollinsPublishers

So Done
Copyright © 2018 by Paula Chase

All rights reserved. No part of this book may be used or reproduced in any manner whatsoever without written permission except in the case of brief quotations embodied in critical articles and reviews. Printed in the United States of America. For information address HarperCollins Children's Books, a division of HarperCollins Publishers, 195 Broadway, New York, NY 10007.
www.harpercollinschildrens.com

The text of this book is set in Garth Graphic. Book design by Sylvie Le Floc'h

Library of Congress Cataloging-in-Publication Data
Names: Chase, Paula, author.
Title: So done / by Paula Chase.
Description: First edition. | New York, NY: Greenwillow Books, an imprint of HarperCollinsPublishers, [2018] | Summary: "When best friends Metai and Jamila are reunited after a summer apart, their friendship threatens to combust from the pressure of secrets, middle school, and looming auditions for a potentially life-changing new talented-and-gifted program"— Provided by publisher.
Identifiers: LCCN 2018022297 | ISBN 9780062691781 (hardback)
Subjects: | CYAC: Best friends—Fiction. | Friendship—Fiction. | Family problems—Fiction. | Middle schools—Fiction. | Schools—Fiction. | African Americans—Fiction. | Racially-mixed people—Fiction. | Auditions—Fiction. | BISAC: JUVENILE FICTION / Social Issues / Friendship. | JUVENILE FICTION / Social Issues / Adolescence. | JUVENILE FICTION / Family / Alternative Family.
Classification: LCC PZ7.C38747 Sk 2018 | DDC [Fic]—dc23 LC record available at https://lccn.loc.gov/2018022297
18 19 20 21 22 CG/LSCH 10 9 8 7 6 5 4 3 2 1

First Edition

Greenwillow Books

*

To Representation . . . it matters!

**

CHAPTER 1

For people keeping score: Metai Johnson didn't need anybody.

Not her father, who acted like he was sixteen years old.

Not her mother, who depending on which Cove rumor you believed, had either been sent back to Korea or was a manager of a hair-supply store her parents (Tai's grandparents) owned somewhere.

Tai didn't know if either were true, and all Nona, her grandmother, would say was, "She not around here, no more."

Tai believed Nona, but she had looked her mother up on FriendMe, anyway. Once . . . maybe twice. Definitely not more than four times. She was sure it was her unless there were a lot of Kim-Tae Yuns out there. The account was locked. So all Tai knew was they had eyes alike and sort of the same kind of name— *tay* not *tie*, she always had to tell people.

But she didn't know if it was really her and she'd stopped caring.

She didn't need anybody.

Just because her heart was doing tiny leaps since she'd noticed that Mr. Jamal's truck was gone already, which meant he'd headed to his sister's to get Bean, which meant Bean would be home soon . . . didn't mean she needed Bean. She just missed her. Missing somebody and needing them weren't the same thing.

She sat on top of her nightstand staring across the small road that separated her row of townhouses from Bean's. She'd been up there all morning, afraid if she moved she'd miss her return. Not that Mr. Jamal would let her come hang out right away. He never did. Even when Tai tried to sweet-talk her way inside for just a few minutes, Mr. Jamal would always say the same thing— "Jamila just got home, Metai. She'll see you tomorrow."

It was the dumbest rule she'd ever heard of.

It didn't stop her from waiting, though. She just wanted to see Bean back, for herself, the second it happened.

The weekends Bean visited her aunt in the Woods were bad enough. Her being ghost all summer was too much. Tai had looked so lame walking to center court by herself. She'd hung out with Rasheeda and Monique, but it got played out, fast.

For one, Mo had a bad habit of always rolling her eyes or scrunching up her mouth when she disagreed with Tai. She also didn't have a problem telling Tai she was overreacting.

Then, Sheeda was just too sometimey. One minute she was 100 percent on your side agreeing, then as soon as Mo so much as opened her mouth to breathe the opposite, Sheeda was skating to the other side. It got on Tai's nerves. Like, girl, pick a side.

Still, the fact was her, Mo, Sheeda, and Bean were a squad. Had been close since fifth grade when the seventh-grade girls in the hood came at them sideways trying to start trouble.

It stopped almost dead once they cliqued, though. The older girls knew Mo and Tai were a match to anybody when it came to clapping back, and if it came to it, knuckling up.

In Tai's mind, she was the leader when they were all hanging together. But without Bean, she realized she was the third wheel. It's why she had faked not feeling well to get out of going to the zoo when they went with the Boys & Girls Club and even to the carnival, her favorite tradition. She wasn't about to sit there looking dumb while Mo and Sheeda shared their little inside jokes. It made her feel like an outsider in the small circle she'd been the head bee of since elementary school.

That wasn't the only thing, though. Bean's absence had left a block of cold anger in Tai's stomach all summer. The closer it got to Bean returning to the hood, the more the anger melted. But it had eaten at Tai that Bean had never once invited her over to the Woods. Not even for a few hours just to chill. Tai couldn't even hint at an invite since Bean had barely texted her, either. And *barely* was being generous.

Like, how do you take a break from being somebody's friend? Tai wondered, the icy annoyance seeping back into her veins. Because that's what it felt like Bean had done. One minute Bean was right there across the street. They were texting, hanging at center court, or chilling at Tai's, like, almost every day. Then bam, Bean was in the Woods and it was like she fell off the earth. At least if she had jumped into the Mini Chat now and then that would have been something, but she had cut everybody off. Who does that?

She stared across the street like a thirsty person eyeing a glass of water, needing to see her friend get out of Mr. Jamal's truck so all the stupid thoughts she'd had all summer would stop. Until Bean was back rolling through the hood with her again, things felt off.

Tai closed her eyes for a second then said the words out loud, "They felt off before she even left."

She pushed the thought out of her mind fast, like it was a bug lighting on her leg. But it made its way back.

She hugged her knees to her chest, her entire body taking up the tiny top of the nightstand, and gave into it. She already knew that the more she tried not to think about it, she would. So she played things over again for the millionth time.

It had been Bean's last night before heading to the Woods. Tai had to nag her for nearly an hour to come hang out because Bean was always worried trouble would start. Definitely if you stepped to somebody wrong in the Cove, you got your bell rung. And if it came to it, sometimes a gun might blow. So, staying in the house was Bean's religion.

Bean had finally come—she always did if Tai bugged her nonstop. But this time, as they were walking out of the house, Bean had mumbled, "So glad I'm leaving tomorrow."

At least Tai was pretty sure that's what she'd said. Bean was really tall—a good six inches taller than four-foot-eleven Tai—so maybe she had just misheard her. Plus, she'd said it really low and her back was to Tai. When she turned around, she had seemed okay. It was crazy.

Tai had debated with herself—had she imagined Bean was mad or not? Then Bean left and hadn't dropped a single "hey" into their group chat with Mo and Sheeda, so Tai knew something had to be up. She started the same text to Bean, five times: *what's up? Is everything okay?*

But it made her look too pressed. She wasn't about that life, so she deleted it every time. And as soon as she did, the urge would hit to text—*u act like u in another country . . . what u can't hit nobody up?* 😊 Anything to get Bean to write back—*lolz* or *sorry been busy*—so Tai would know everything was still cool. And the longer summer wore on without a word, it definitely felt like something was wrong, like they were beefing but Tai didn't know over what. It wasn't like her and Bean ever fought—not really. Not unless you counted the times she changed Bean's mind about staying in the house. *That* they "fought" over plenty. But that would have been dumb. Every time she successfully got Bean out the house, they had a good time. What was to be mad over?

An answer popped into her head. Something that had happened in her backyard. It was stupid. Most things that involved her father were. That's exactly why Tai had (mostly) forgotten about it. And she'd told Bean to do the same thing after it happened. Her father wasn't worth spending energy on. But she couldn't shake it because she was almost sure that Bean hadn't started acting funny until after. A few times she'd come close to asking was Bean mad at her because of it, but Bean knew how her father was. That couldn't have been it.

Could it?

Anger welled in her chest. She couldn't stand her father sometimes. He was forever messing up and Nona was forever forgiving him. Bean knew that, since she was who Tai ranted to anytime he'd done something new to get his stupid butt in trouble. No way Bean was mad at her because of him.

Convinced, she stamped thoughts of it back like you did a roach you were trying to scare away because all the thinking and wondering stopped today. Bean was coming back.

The cartwheels in her stomach settled. She let her eyes drift to her mirror. She approved of the honey-complexioned cutie with light green oval-shaped eyes staring back at her. For good or bad, her icy mint eyes were the one feature she shared with her father.

She sat up, stretching her short torso as far as it would go, checking her profile. She was bootylicious curvy. Wavy jet-black hair ran to the middle of her back on one side. The other side was shaved down. She patted at the soft down absently, still not used to feeling scalp. Bean hadn't seen her new do. Tai hoped she'd love it. Maybe she could get Bean to change up from the braids she always wore and get a matching style.

Her phone dinged softly.

Her grin spread so her entire face was teeth. It was Rollie and his message was classic him—simple, almost boring: *heard ur girl be back on da block today*

She wanted to go in on him for not hitting her up sooner. Then reminded herself what was important was that two weeks ago, her crush since fifth grade was finally acting like he had eyes in his head and could see she was the baddest chick on their block. True, they had mostly talked about TAG, the new talented and gifted program. He played drums and was trying out for the music program. So every text turned to that or him asking was she hyped to try out for TAG dance. She didn't care, though. At least he was hitting her up.

The text sat a few more minutes as she stared across the street counting in her head. When she reached one hundred, she hit him back: *yasss! Finally!*

Roll-Oh: *Can't believe it but u pressed. Ahaaa* 😸

Rollie was the only person in the world that could call her pressed without getting clapped back. At least for now. Things were too fragile for her to get in her feelings about every little thing he teased her about.

DatGirlTai: *Hardly. Mr. Jamal ain't gon let her come out 2day anyway. So its not like I'm gon see her* 😾

Roll-Oh: *he strict as hell huh?*

DatGirlTai: *He just really into family time.* 😴 *But Mr. J all right*

Roll-Oh: *yeah I can't hate. He used to ball up w/ us on the court sometimes when JJ be out there. He cool peoples*

Tai's fingers itched to text back and ask him what was up. Were they becoming a couple? Or was he really texting her just to announce Bean was back today? The whole hood knew that by now. Some people had a newspaper. The Cove had gossip.

After ten minutes she gave in and texted back.

DatGirlTai: *What u up to 2day?*

Her heart smiled when he answered back fast like he'd been waiting on the question.

Roll-Oh: *Rat-a-tat-tat* 🥁

DatGirlTai: *Thas whas up. When u start ur band don't be caught up in groupie chicks* 🙁

Roll-Oh: *LOL groupies da best part of being in a band*

DatGirlTai: *Eww u grimy. I might have to stop messin w/u* 😛

It was the closest she'd ever come to admitting that she was into him. Even as she hoped he would take it like a joke, she wanted him to admit the same.

Roll-Oh: *So u could stop talking to me jus like dat?* 😕 *Wow. Much shade*

She flirted back, encouraged by his answer.

DatGirlTai: *Oh so it matter if I cut u off? That's more like it. #BettaCare* ☺

But the convo was over the way it always was—nothing for a few seconds, then minutes. It was the only way she ever knew he was done. It was another reason she was glad Bean was back. She'd let Rollie occupy every corner of her mind. He smothered every other thought. It wasn't cool.

The whump of a door closing snatched her attention from the phone. Mr. Jamal's truck sat in the small driveway.

Her girl was home.

Her fingers texted in a blaze: *Welcome back to the block wench!*

CHAPTER 2

Jamila Phillips was anything but excited to be back home. *Curious* was a better word. Something had told her her dad and brothers were somewhat of a mess without her. But when she walked through the door and saw the house clean and Jeremy, her eight-year-old brother, still alive and unbruised after a summer with their older brother, JJ, even curiosity wore off.

Between Tai's welcome back text and the mandatory game of Spades with her dad and brothers—her dad's attempt at family time—an entire summer was already starting to feel like wisps of a dream. She missed Aunt

Jacqi, her sister, Cinny, and the small three-bedroom house in the Woods already.

JJ and Jeremy's bickering didn't help.

"You can't play that card. You said you was out of hearts." JJ's head rose above the cards in his hand as he tried to peek at Jeremy's. He was too competitive when it came to playing Spades, or anything for that matter.

Jeremy snatched his elbows off the table, hiding his cards. "Stop trying to look, JJ." He pouted. "You don't know what cards I have." He looked to Mila and their dad for help. Their dad stayed silent, letting them work it out. Seeing he was on his own, Jeremy put a little weight in his voice. "I can play that card. Bean just played a heart."

JJ sucked his teeth. "Two plays back you cut hearts with a spade. You can't do that." Seeing Jeremy's face crinkle in confusion, JJ's face went through a dozen versions of annoyance. He laid his cards down, careful not to slam them—that would get their dad involved in a hurry—as he argued his case. "See, man, Nut still don't know how play. Daddy, tell him he reneging."

Mila could tell Jeremy's feelings were hurt by the way his lip pooched, but he held off whining. Rubbing his shoulder, she leaned over, talking low.

"Remember how we said you should only use spades if you don't have the suit being played or if spades leads?"

Jeremy kept his cards on his lap, checked them out, then nodded hesitantly. JJ made a *prrfft* noise as he sighed. He slid down in his seat, arms folded, but wisely stayed quiet.

Mila looked down. Jeremy had definitely reneged. He did it all the time. Anybody with Jeremy on their team lost, which meant JJ never wanted him to be his partner. Which meant Jeremy's feelings got hurt right out of the gate.

She hated how rough JJ was on him.

"That's enough," her dad said. He stretched and landed his long arms on both JJ and Mila's shoulders. He pulled them toward him in an awkward hug. "This little moment of togetherness was brought to you courtesy of Dad. Welcome back to the asylum, baby girl." He kissed Mila on the forehead then lightly knocked skulls with JJ before lecturing, "I'll go over the finer points of Spades with Nut later. But you don't need to be so hard on him, Jamal Jr."

Mila and Jeremy shared a smile. JJ hated when their dad went full-name on him. He sucked it up as their dad continued. "First of all, it's just a game. Second of all, you getting mad over it is only teaching him how to be a bad sport. Do better."

He stood up, towering over his son. His light brown eyes were soft around the edges. The lecture was mild advice, not a forewarning to punishment.

"Yes, sir," JJ said, full of attitude that their dad thankfully ignored.

Jamal Sr. sidestepped his way around the coffee table. "Come on, Nut. Help me make your sister a welcome-home dinner."

"Can it be spaghetti?" Jeremy asked, running after him.

Out of habit, Mila gathered the cards and started cleaning up. She wasn't hungry, but there was no point in sharing that. Her brothers were always hungry, especially Jeremy.

"Y'all keep letting Nut play wrong and he gon' end up getting his feelings hurt when he play with other people," JJ said. He scooted his cards toward Mila with a flick of his fingers. "You know how people get about playing Spades. They take it serious."

His face was screwed up in what Mila called his "harder than you" look. He'd started doing it at the end of the school year. It was annoying, not just because it was ugly looking but it made Mila scared that he was trying to be like too many other dudes in the Cove—all about proving they weren't afraid of anything. Part of her got it. In their neighborhood, one minute somebody could have your back. But then, if your back weighed theirs down, it was every boy and girl for themselves.

The fact was, sometimes friendships in the Cove were like a magic trick—now you see 'em . . . now you don't. Mila couldn't get used to that, but JJ, a year older and supposedly wiser than her, rolled with the way things were around their block. She just hoped it wouldn't ever make him too rough.

She took her time collecting the cards, tapping them on the table every few seconds so her stack stayed neat.

JJ folded his long arms across his chest, staring at her, challenging her. She'd been home for exactly three hours and already they were bumping heads—which in JJ language was having a conversation.

She put a rubber band around the cards. "I was trying to explain the rules to him. But by then you'd already hurt his feelings," Mila said. "You know once his feelings hurt, he not even listening anymore."

JJ shrugged. "Yeah, well, ain't nobody out there

in the hood gonna care about his feelings being hurt."
There was an angry glint in his eye. He seemed ready
to say something else. Instead he sighed and put his
hand out.

Mila looked at his empty hand, confused. He shook
his hand at her. "Give me the cards, man. I'mma put
'em away."

Mila laughed. "You act like I should have known
that. When was the last time you ever helped clean
up?"

JJ rolled his eyes but he cracked a smile. He plucked
the cards out of her hand and stored them in a wooden
box next to the sofa. Mila sat on one end of the sofa
and he sat two cushions down from her. They looked
like two people on an awkward first date waiting for
their chaperone to sit in between. His long legs were
stretched out off to the side of the large coffee table.
When their dad wasn't home, he kicked his feet up on
the table. But he knew better now.

The clank of pots and pans and the flow of running
water came from the kitchen. Jeremy was asking their
dad a million questions.

JJ looked Mila up and down like he was taking
inventory.

"Dang, Bean, did you even eat at Aunt Jacqs'? You even skinnier than normal," he said gruffly. It was also a peace offering.

Mila rubbed her arms, feeling how lean they were but loving the new muscle she felt on them. A long time ago some Captain Obvious had started calling her "Bean," short for "beanpole." Like hood nicknames did, it stuck. She promised herself she'd stop calling Jeremy "Nut," short for "peanut." She had no idea if it bothered him. It didn't matter. It bothered her and she was on a mission to get as many people to call her by her real name as she could. Hopefully it would trickle down to everybody, but correcting JJ would only cause another disagreement. She let it slide.

"We just ate whatever. Aunt Jacqs kept plenty of food in the house, though."

"Ouno how you stayed the whole summer," JJ said with a frown. "It's too quiet over there for me. The Cove is better."

Arguing with JJ was always pointless. After a few minutes he'd start lobbing insults just to have something to say. Mila had seen it get so bad between him and Cinny, their older sister, that it turned into a fight. She and Jeremy usually just walked out of his face.

Besides, she didn't know how to explain that she wasn't into standing up for their hood like it needed soldiers. It was annoying how so many people in the Cove were only about loyalty, repping their spot and dreaming big even if actually getting out of the Cove was only a dream.

Plus, being a girl in the Cove was different from being a boy. Boys played ball and hung out side by side whether they really liked each other or not. Mila, on the other hand, had spent most of elementary school and her first two years of middle school avoiding the petty beefs that stirred up among the girls in their hood.

It was tiring having to watch everything you said and worrying if something innocent would turn into a grudge, a push in the hallway, then an all-out brawl.

She knew JJ would disagree. To him, it was normal to step to somebody if they disrespected you. More than normal, it was practically Cove law.

Everything wasn't that simple. But she couldn't say that. If she did, he'd ask questions that she didn't want to answer. She might even end up admitting why she'd gone to stay over at their aunt's in the first place. Or she might finally explode over how stupid it was that being quiet in the Cove got you picked on, talked about, or worse. Her and Jeremy were quiet. It wasn't because they couldn't stand up for themselves, it was because quiet was easier than drama.

She settled for a simple admission. "I loved it over Aunt Jacqs'."

"Puh I guess so. Me and Jeremy had to pick up your slack." He pushed his hand at her, snatching it away as Mila swatted at it. "You can't be leaving me to be the house mother no more."

The term "house mother" was hilarious. JJ was anything but. Still, him reminding Mila that she was expected to play Little Mama to their brother made her hot.

Seemed like everybody had an opinion about her going to the Woods for the summer. Yet, nobody had ever asked her why she'd been so anxious to go. Not JJ. Not Tai. Even their dad assumed she just needed a break from a house full of males. And she hadn't let him think anything different. Hadn't wanted him to. Still, it was like nobody ever thought about what she wanted.

It weighed on her mind through dinner as her dad lobbed question after question about life with Aunt Jacqs. She found herself faking cheer as the conversation swung between what she did there and JJ's bizarre list of why none of it could be better than home.

When dinner was over, Mila escaped to the wonderful silence of her own room. She already missed how her dad's younger sister would stand in the doorway of Mila's bedroom with her arms crossed like she was about to be stern while her face beamed. "What you up to, Miss Jamila?" she'd ask. Before Mila could answer she'd keep right on talking, "Come on, let's go . . ." and then she'd name their activity for the day—try to plant vegetables, hit the nail salon, or take a long walk to the plaza down the street. Whatever the suggestion, Mila never felt like she had a choice in whether she wanted to go or not. But she didn't mind. Aunt Jacqs always picked fun stuff to do.

She looked over at her bedroom doorway half expecting Aunt Jacqs to be there. Instead, the voices of her brothers floated from their room sharp and loud.

"You got crushed, punk," JJ said.

"You cheating," Jeremy said, barely holding back the whine.

Mila got up and shut her door and sat in the middle of the floor cross-legged.

It was time for some changes. She couldn't change

the Cove or even JJ, but she could change her room. She mindscaped a few ideas. Take the bunk beds down. Move the desk out. Put cubes for shoes and school supplies where the desk was. Get one of those bouncy trampoline chairs. Ideas raced in and out.

She stretched out her arms. Her fingers bumped into the frame of her and Cinny's bunk beds on one side and the clunky wooden desk on the other, making it official—none of her ideas would work. There wasn't enough space.

She laid back on the floor and stared up at the ceiling. Sometimes when she did that, ideas came together like puzzle pieces. She wasn't aware she'd closed her eyes until her phone vibrated.

DatGirlTai: *can u come over tomorrow when ur father let u off lockdown?* 😬

Tai had asked her the same question a million times. By now Mila's fingers could have typed back "sure" or "yeah" without her even thinking about it. But she wouldn't let them. She held the phone tight until the slim edge bit into the flesh of her fingers. A wave of guilt and fear made her feel dizzy.

How could she be afraid to go to her own best friend's house?

She was a second too late clapping her mind shut against the memories that answered the question. Then immediately a slideshow of the good times they had at Tai's also played in her head, making her feel worse. When they weren't at school or dance they were at Tai's, because at Mila's there were rules. Rules she got tired of defending against Tai's rolling eyes and rants of "How come your father won't let us do this?" and "Why can't we do that?"

The other thing was, at Mila's house either Jeremy was underfoot or JJ was warring with Tai about anything just to have something to say. Mila had finally figured out that JJ was flirting with Tai and Tai was definitely flirting back. It got on Mila's nerves. Not only did she get tired of them going at each other, fussing, but the thought of her brother and best friend starting a ship was ick.

At Tai's, Mila didn't have to worry about that. Also, hanging there made her feel grown: her and Tai cooking themselves lunch or watching whatever they wanted on the TV, even sneaking to one of the channels Ms. Sophia thought she had locked until Mila panicked and begged Tai to turn it before they got caught.

Tai's house was where they had tried on makeup. Where they had locked themselves in the bathroom when Tai found a condom, so they could see what it looked like.

Then Tai's father had ruined it.

At first Mila still tried going over there like everything was good. She laughed at their same old jokes when she really wanted to look over her shoulder and make sure Mr. Bryant wasn't lurking. When he was home, usually lying on the sofa asleep or watching TV, she scooted up the stairs fast so he wouldn't notice her. But doing that made her stomach gurgle like she was going to have the runs. *That's* why she had asked to stay at Aunt Jacqs'. She couldn't stand the thought of spending the entire summer making up excuses to avoid going across the street.

Now what was she supposed to do? If she stopped going to Tai's, her dad would notice. And if he noticed, he'd—what had Aunt Jacqs called what her dad did? Mind art. He'd paint his own picture of what people were thinking. And he usually got what they were thinking right.

Goose bumps raised on her arms. Her dad did it all the time to her and her siblings. And Mila could do it a little, too. She'd just never put a name to it until her aunt did.

If her dad ever connected Mr. Bryant with her wanting to go away over the summer, it wouldn't be good. Not at all. Still, she had no intentions of going to Tai's house. Not yet. She had things to think through.

She texted back, fingers trembling so much she had to retype the short message twice before it was right.

doubt it. Been gone all summer, have chores 😠

Keeping the house clean was definitely one of her dad's many rules. So the text could have been true. She laid the phone down with a clunk, like telling the lie made it too heavy to hold.

She'd so be in trouble if Tai ever became a mind artist.

CHAPTER
3

Tai called for Bean three times. The only answer was the blaring of the TV. She pressed her face against the door's screen, trying to see inside. "Where everybody at? Helloooo?"

"Girl, stop hollering up in my house," JJ commanded, mouth full of sandwich. He emerged from the kitchen shirtless and sat down on the sofa without inviting Tai in.

"You so ignorant, JJ. Like you can't even just say *come in*?" Her eyes lingered on his bare chest before straining to peer up the dim stairwell. "Bean ready?"

"How I'm supposed to know?" he asked, turning the TV up.

If Mr. Jamal were home, the TV wouldn't be so loud. Tai burst through the front door. Hands on her hips, she shook her head at JJ, pretending to be more disgusted than she was. With his light brown eyes and dimpled cheeks, he was fine. There was a time when she'd imagined being his girlfriend. What could be more perfect than dating the boy across the street and her best friend's brother?

She'd caught him staring at her butt a few times. So she knew he thought she was cute. But sometimes JJ was so mean to her, Tai wondered if she could be wrong about some of his sly glances. She always made sure to diss him as hard as he did her just in case their light beefing was real.

"You a trip," she muttered.

A loud gasp and the patter of Bean racing down the steps cut her off from laying him out more.

"Oh my God, Tai, it's even cuter in person." Mila's fingers ran over the shaved area of Tai's head. "No bun for you."

The side that was still long flowed past Tai's ear in black waves. The short side was shaved to a down softness, the top layered in tight barrels that curlicued at the ends, disobeying the rigid rows.

"Noelle probably gonna be annoyed, huh?" Tai snorted. The new hairstyle would be one more thing that made her stand out, in a bad way, in dance class. It wasn't like she was ever going to be a real ballerina. But their dance teacher kept trying. She was constantly on Tai for everything from her arms being in the wrong place to her not wearing the right clothes—black leotard and pink tights for ballet, any colored leotard and nude tights for jazz.

Whatever.

Bean fluffed the long part, trying to solve the issue aloud. "You might be able to make some kind of lopsided pony."

"Hmph. It's not like I run around getting my hair styled to please her," Tai said, annoyed out of habit. She folded her arms, eyes rolling. "Noelle just need take a sip of get over it."

Bean gave her much side eye, then laughed. "You gon' tell her that next class?"

Tai couldn't help laughing. Bean knew she was all talk. For as much as Tai hated ballet, she craved Noelle's praise. She never did much to earn it and it killed her that she even cared, but she did a little.

"I'm going out for a while," Mila hollered over the TV. "Don't leave Jeremy by his self."

JJ made a face at her but nodded just the same.

"Why the cute ones always gotta be ignorant?" Tai asked, loud, smiling JJ's way as they walked out.

"One day JJ really gonna hurt your feelings if you keep coming for him," Mila said as they stepped into the late summer heat.

"Ain't nobody scared of your brother, girl." Tai flicked a look back on the house. "Besides, we just playing anyway. JJ cool with me."

As they walked the hood, Tai was determined to fill Bean in on everything that had happened. Every step they took deeper into the Cove together made her heart beat with pride. How could Bean think the boring burbs was better?

Pirates Cove was one of four low-income projects in Del Rio Bay. It was a jungle of twenty building units erupting from tar-black streets. Each unit had ten two-level attached row homes: narrow, tall, and identical except for their different-colored doors. It was home to more than seven hundred people, some Latino, but most Black, all of them poor by Del Rio Bay standards.

Just like the name suggested, the neighborhood was an inlet, well hidden from the nicer parts of the city. People could drive past its long tree-lined entrance and never know a neighborhood humming with activity lay beyond it.

Cove life centered around the row house stoop, the rec center, and the basketball courts. And if you needed quick groceries or a bite to eat, the Wa was a short walk through a wooded path, along with a laundry mat, an L-store, and a nail salon. As far as Tai was concerned, the hood had everything she needed, especially now that Bean was back.

Music thumped out of open windows and from cars being washed. People sat on their front stoops, on the phone or catching the midday sun. Kids on scooters and bikes or running raced past, heading toward center court, the heart of the hood where the playground, basketball court, and rec center beckoned. Tai filled her lungs with the energy.

They passed a slender dude, wearing a baby blue wave cap, leaning against a light pole—Rock Jensen. He looked bored, like he was debating whether to hold the pole up or move along. A silver Acura slow crept up to him. He nodded at them like he was saying hey.

The Acura slowly wheeled a block away and stopped. Tai knew that in a second a boy, her age or younger, would roll up to the car window and slide the driver a package, then slink off to wait for the signal again.

Rock was the only dealer determined not to be intimidated by Mr. Jamal and his keep-drugs-out-of-our-hood attitude. It didn't matter how many times Bean's father appealed to his neighbors to turn in anybody they saw selling drugs in the neighborhood, Rock found ways to disrespect his attempts to keep the Cove clean.

Bean was scared of Rock. So Tai chattered on and sped up to get past him. Of course, to make sure they saw him, Rock smiled and swiped two fingers against his forehead in a salute. Bean's long legs sped up another notch.

When Tai glanced back, Rock was on his phone, no longer looking their way. She made light of it by patting her chest in dramatic relief. "Oh, whew. So the Woods didn't totally change you."

"What are you talking about?" Mila asked, looking over her shoulder.

"I see you still scared of Rock. So you still the same old Bean." She laughed to ease Bean's mind. She didn't need her friend finding more reasons to hate on their hood.

Bean shrugged, playing along. "Rock is crazy. So you're the one a little off for not being scared of him."

"You know I'm lo-co," Tai called out, jiggling her head.

They laughed at the inside joke. The warmth of the moment made Tai want to hug herself. It was good to be walking with Bean instead of by herself. She was about to admit it when Bean said, "Tai, look . . . can you please stop calling me 'Bean'?"

Tai stopped in her tracks. "We been calling you that for years. I mean, it's your name."

"No, it's my nickname." Mila frowned. "And I walk around in this body every day. I don't need everybody reminding me how skinny I am."

"You act like you hate it," Tai said, eyebrow raised.

"I do," Bean said. Her hand wandered to her hair and twirled a random braid. A habit she had when she was nervous or scared. Tai figured it meant Bean was going to back down, but she didn't. "Plus we're thirteen years old. We're too old for nicknames like that."

Tai cut her eyes. "You mean you are. Everybody don't have a problem with it."

Mila sucked her teeth. "You mean like Simp. You really think he likes being called that?"

Tai couldn't believe they were seriously talking about this. Who cared about Simp? He was their age but still in sixth grade. A fact that didn't seem to embarrass him at all. Tai wasn't sure he could be embarrassed. God knew she tried every chance she got and the boy wasn't fazed.

His real name was Deontae. He had a massive head full of dreads and his hairline came down too far, like somebody had taped it too close to his eyebrows. All that hair—eyebrows and hairline together—made it seem like he was always squinting, trying to figure things out. And it made him look like he wasn't real bright.

Simp didn't help himself, either. He blurted out whatever, like he didn't know better what thoughts to keep to himself. It made people come right back at him when he said something they didn't like. Tai was about to point that out when Bean snorted.

"Tai come on. 'Simp' is short for 'simple.' He probably hates it but you know him . . . he just rolls with it."

"And he too simple to know better," Tai said. She

threw her hands up. "And that's the point. Nicknames be fitting people. You are who you are, Bean."

"Okay," Mila said, and Tai thought she was ready to give in until she folded her arms and said, "So you would be cool if everybody called you Chinky because of your eyes?"

"Well, that would be ignorant and racist," Tai said with a hollow attempt at laughing. She really didn't want to argue, so she made fun of herself. "I wouldn't like it but you act like people don't say that behind my back." She play-whispered, "Yeah, you know Tai . . . that girl with the chinky eyes."

"That's not to your face," Mila said sharply. "And it's different than them giving you a whole name because of it. You don't know how it feels."

"And you get in your feelings about the littlest things," Tai said. She couldn't believe Bean had just snapped on her. Was this really happening? She started walking again, flip-flops smacking hard against her feet as she tried to sort it all out in her head.

First Bean went to the Woods for the whole summer. She didn't send text one the entire time. Now she was being all brand-new wanting people to stop calling her something they'd called her forever. It was too much.

She waited for Bean to say "never mind" or something to signal it wasn't a big deal. If she did, Tai promised herself she'd give in—say sorry back, call her what she wanted. She wasn't *trying* to ruin their first time hanging out. But only if Bean said something first. That's how it always worked.

They walked in silence. The quiet was a weight on Tai's head.

They passed third court. In a few minutes they'd be near center court, where the squad was waiting and everybody would see them mad at each other. Tai didn't want that. Not now, when she finally had her sidekick back, riding with her.

Something told her Mo would have plenty to say about them arguing already. How many times had they all been together and the word *petty* had been thrown out there to describe Tai? It was all supposed to be a joke, but Mo had used the word five times too many for Tai. She could call herself petty. Because sometimes she was petty. You had to be toward some people. But the real was, she didn't want Bean thinking she was being petty.

She coached herself: *It's her name. I don't care what she want people to call her. Just say you'll do it. Just say it.*

She snuck a peek, hoping to see Bean pouting. It would mean she was just as upset as Tai was about them fussing. Then Tai could save the day by just giving in and making everything right again. But Bean's face was a stony mask of anger.

Tai couldn't remember a single time she'd seen Bean genuinely mad. Until that very moment, she didn't even know her best friend could get mad. It sounded dumb but it was true. And it was scary. She fumbled to say something that would erase it.

"I ain't making no promises. But I'll try," she declared. In her head it sounded way nicer than how it actually came out. But it was out. She'd done it. She'd been the bigger person, i.e., the opposite of petty. Take that, Mo.

She breathed slowly through her nose to stop her racing heart from leaping out of her chest. It was over. She could finally fill Bean—Mila? Jamila? Tai couldn't decide—in on her and Rollie. She'd been dying to ask her whether their ship name should be RollTai or MeTollie. She turned to share her thoughts and saw Bean roll her eyes up toward the sky and mouth, "Gee, thanks."

She mouthed the words so hard Tai swore she'd actually heard them.

She was still staring at her when Bean finally looked her way.

"Yeah, all right," she said. And it sounded like she was forcing herself just like Tai had forced herself to give in to Bean's request.

The lackluster response took the wind out of Tai. She felt like she was walking down the street with a stranger. But in three minutes they'd be at the rec. Everybody would be happy to see . . . Mila. Tai would look crazy standing there with a stank face as the world welcomed back her best friend. So she did something she had never done before—she played like she hadn't seen Mila's reaction. She talked on and on, about Rollie, heard herself laugh, and was more grateful than she would ever admit when Bean . . . Mila (whatever) laughed back.

At the end of the day, she'd convinced herself that it wasn't a big deal after all. It couldn't be. They still had a few weeks left of summer. Her girl was back home. And her and Rollie were this close to becoming (she and Bean decided) MeTollie.

Things weren't just back to normal, they were better than normal.

CHAPTER
4

Monday morning Mila was up early. She heard her dad walking through the hall softly, trying not to wake anybody. It was only 5:30 a.m., an hour earlier than he usually got up, which meant it was his day to open the auto repair shop where he was a supervisor. She lay still, readjusting to the sounds of the house through the thin walls—her dad creaking down the stairs, JJ's light snoring next door, and Jeremy's feet kicking furiously at something, then calming.

After hearing the door close behind her dad, she lay there, hoping sleep would return. But her brain was up and ready to go and thinking about yesterday's walk with Tai through the hood. She'd surprised herself over how angry she'd been. Her anger had lit in her chest like a match to gasoline. She'd been close to returning home—her mood ruined—then shocked when Tai agreed to stop calling her "Bean." If you could call somebody saying they'd "try" as agreeing. That was classic Tai and enough for Mila. As quickly as the anger flared, it had blown out and, thankfully, the rest of the afternoon had been fine.

Even though she'd enjoyed strolling the hood more than usual—mainly because she hadn't done it in so long—she still didn't get why Tai loved wandering from one court to the other so much. The goal was usually to run into Roland or meet up in front of the rec or at the basketball court with Mo and Sheeda. It always felt like they were walking in circles. But anything was better than being over at Tai's house.

Mila made her way down the stairs, skipping over the step that squeaked. Sun bathed the living room in light. The room felt so much bigger when they weren't all in it. She sat in the corner of the couch with her long legs curled to her chest as the sun crept farther into the room, warming her. She was back home whether she liked it or not, wanted to be or not.

Whether the Cove was the worst or best place to live depended on who you asked or what newspaper you read. The *DRB Daily* said the crime activity in the Cove was a blemish on the city. Mila had asked her dad what a blemish was. She was only eight at the time, Jeremy's age. At thirteen she was more familiar with blemishes than she wanted to be, but back then it was a new word.

She learned two things that day: that a blemish was a flaw that spoiled how something looked and that when it came to anything the paper said about their hood, it instantly turned her dad into a ghetto professor. He wasn't behind a podium like a professor, but standing in front of the sink washing up the dishes from dinner, he lectured like one.

He plucked the paper from Mila's hand and skimmed the article. His mouth twisted like someone had rubbed lemon on his lips. "The *Daily* takes one fact, adds in fifteen opinions, and calls it news." He had slammed the paper onto the table, ignoring Mila's outstretched hand, then changed his mind. He lifted it back up to his face, lips moving as he continued reading. He waved the paper as he talked. Droplets of water from his still damp hands sprinkled Mila. "It's not like I want people driving through our neighborhood like it's a zoo, to check it out for themselves, but I'm tired of the paper making folk think a bunch of thugs are lying in wait for anybody that gets near the entrance." His eyes glowed. He fixed them on Mila, his lone student, and she had gazed up at him. What her dad said was king. When he got like this—and that was anytime somebody attacked the Cove—she found herself curious but also afraid of his passion. The only other thing he spoke about with that much energy was her, Cinny, and her brothers. It's how she knew he loved their neighborhood, "blemish" or not.

His eyes softened but his words had been firm. "The sad part is most of the nonsense that goes on here only hurts the people living here. They don't need to be unnecessarily scaring folks away." With that, the anger dissolved. He laid the paper down on the table. His fingers were black with newsprint but he hadn't seemed to care. He opened his arms and pulled Mila into a hug. "Listen to me, Jamila. It's a lot of knuckleheads in the Cove but it's way more good people here who just can't afford to live nowhere else. The paper don't care to learn the difference." His stomach ballooned then caved as he sighed. He stepped back so she could see his face. "We're all either criminals or victims to them. But that doesn't mean it's true. There's plenty good in the hood. Plenty." He pecked her on the forehead and went back to washing dishes. Lecture over.

Mila never did finish reading the article. And the thing she never told her dad was that what little she had read she agreed with. There was crime in the Cove. There was drug dealing. There were fights and even shootings sometimes. She didn't really understand why her dad defended it so much. She wasn't really sure what part of the article he disagreed with. But what she did know was that because of her dad constantly trying to improve their nabe, everybody in the Cove knew not to mess with her and her siblings, at least when it came to offering them drugs or asking them to join anything even closely resembling a gang. Mila was probably one of the safest people in their hood because people knew if her dad suspected someone was robbing, stealing, dealing, or vandalizing, he had no problem confronting them or even turning them. So when people saw her and her brothers, they mostly played it straight. Except people like Rock Jensen.

She shuddered thinking about his two-finger salute. It was like he'd purposely saluted to make sure she saw him, low-key daring her to go back and tell her dad she'd seen him dealing drugs in broad daylight. For all the good her dad saw in the Cove, people like Rock were why she chose to stay in the house when she wasn't at the rec's Open Play nights or at dance. She wasn't afraid of the neighborhood, really. She just hated drama, whether it was petty gossiping, constant instigating, or some random fight breaking out. Avoiding it was hard. She'd seen a girl get jumped for not saying *thank you* loud enough after Samyra said the girl's shoes were cute. It got that bad sometimes.

So she watched what she said and who she said it to. She was content to be in the house.

Could she do that forever? Probably not. But she did have a plan. It was actually more of an idea, and as soon as JJ got up she wanted to see what he thought about it. He got on her nerves sometimes, but without Cinny he was her only hope when she needed advice. She prayed he wouldn't sleep all day.

Normally she'd want the boys to stay asleep as long as possible. Once they were up, the TV never went off. For now the large flat-screen, a Christmas gift from her dad to the whole family, was a blank black eye. She turned her head and watched her murky reflection in it.

Her siblings shared their light brown skin with her dad. She was a dark-skinned beauty (no blemishes this month) who looked more like her mother than any of them. She hadn't seen her mother in years. Tried not to think about her much. Braids escaped from the fat bun on top of her head. No matter how many bands she put on it, it was impossible to tame every braid. They were too skinny and too many. Her eyes were wide and brown, always curious but also quick to lower to avoid challenging or being challenged.

"Good morning, Jamila," she whispered to her image.

"Bean, why you saying good morning to yourself?" Jeremy's sleepy voice asked.

"Nut, you scared me," she said as her legs shot out in alarm. She scooped them in and sat cross-legged, making room for her brother. "I was just playing around."

Jeremy sat beside her close enough to be in her lap. Her heart swelled with love for him. Her younger brother was a sweetie. She wished he could stay that way. But being sweet and living in the Cove wasn't a good match. She knew that too well. He stretched out and laid his head on her crossed ankles.

He talked through a yawn. "Did Daddy leave any money so we can walk up to the Wa?"

Mila scratched lightly at his scalp. Something she'd done when he was a baby to get him to sleep. "I'm not sure. I haven't been in the kitchen yet."

Jeremy's day was made whenever Daddy left them change for a chili dog or candy at the convenience store at the mouth of their neighborhood. All he thought about was food. Mila didn't blame him. JJ was all about swiping food off his plate. No doubt it was some stupid test to toughen him up.

"I'm glad you back home. JJ sleep too long and I don't always want cereal," Jeremy said. He lay looking up into Mila's face. "Is it true that Daddy gon' send you to live with Aunt Jacqs like he did Cinny?"

Mila laid her hands on his warm cheeks and rubbed softly. "Who told you that? JJ?" She smiled at Jeremy's eager head nod. "I'm not going nowhere. You know how JJ is."

Jeremy's face brightened. "He said once you left I was gonna have to man up and stop being a baby." He poked his lip out. "I ain't no baby. It's not my fault Daddy won't let me use the stove yet."

Mila laughed. Of course it was about food.

"It's not. But I'mma teach you how to cook this year. You getting too old for everybody to have to cook for you." She said it gently. He seemed to understand. She wiggled her ankle. "You putting my leg to sleep, boop."

He hopped up. "Sorry, Bean." His eyes wandered to the kitchen. She waited on a meal request, willing to fulfill it. She hadn't cooked for him in a while. "Can I go make myself some cereal?" he asked.

"Um-huh," she said, surprised. She rubbed at the prickling needles in her legs. "Hey, Jeremy, can you do me a favor?"

He nodded before even knowing what it was. It made Mila happy and sad at the same time. He was too trusting. It made her want to protect him even more.

"Can you stop calling me 'Bean'?" She explained quickly. "I'm just getting too old for it. I want to be called Mila. And if you want, I can stop calling you 'Nut.'"

His mouth hung open. Then his eyebrows furrowed. His head shook furiously. "No, you can call me that. But, okay." He started to walk away then turned back to her. "Don't get mad if I forget sometimes, okay?"

"I won't," she promised. She tugged gently at his

finger. He was getting too old for sappy hugs from her.
At least that was one less person calling her "Bean." But
now she had a new problem.

Stupid JJ. He had to stop always teasing Jeremy
like that, getting him all worked up. It wasn't right.
Worse, she had been planning to ask JJ if he thought
Daddy would ever send her to live with Aunt Jacqs. It
was the only way she would ever get away from the
endless drama of the Cove and more importantly, going
over to Tai's. But she couldn't ask now after promising
Jeremy she wasn't going anywhere. She was back at
one, without a plan.

CHAPTER
5

The only other place, besides home, Mila felt okay being 100 percent herself was La Maison de la Danse. It was a fancy name for a single room in the rec center walled with mirrors, with a dance bar and an MP3 player dock. The studio was the brainchild of a few parents—her dad one of them—determined to show the Cove's young girls that there was more to dancing than booty popping and gyrating. When it started, there had been twenty girls. Now it was down to nine. The older girls had lost interest when they realized La May didn't teach "video" dancing.

Mila had picked up ballet moves quickly as though someone had taught her in a dream, and she'd awakened at La May ready to go. Jazz was a different story. All the shaking and shimmying made her feel like everybody was staring at her. Which was why Tai liked it, in Mila's opinion. They had only been dancing for two years. It was a fact she was both proud and ashamed of. Proud because Mademoiselle Remy made it clear that for only two years, Mila was very good. Ashamed because she felt like a baby giraffe taking its first steps whenever Mademoiselle pushed her to do something that any other thirteen-year-old dancer would do effortlessly. But it only made her work harder.

She couldn't wait for dance to start. She loved it. And she kept that to herself, thank you very much. She had never admitted that dancing made her feel like she was breathing easier, even to her dad, because he had a habit of taking any small thing her and her brothers liked and blowing it up.

One year she asked to run track. Sprinting looked fun. Only from a distance, as it turned out. But her dad got so excited he bought Mila a pair of sixty-dollar running shoes. He had never bought them any one thing that cost that much. Even her brothers' basketball shoes. Track was cool until her first meet. The thing lasted six hours under the blazing sun and she was only in two events, one at the beginning of the meet, the other at the end. It was instant hate but she didn't have the heart to tell her dad. She finished the season hoping to never sign up again. Then he mentioned coaching the team the next year, forcing her to admit the truth. Cinny ended up sporting the purple and black track shoes for fashion. So it wasn't a total loss.

The prospect of returning to class made her feel like doing pirouettes. She weeded out her dingy, holey, or too-small leotards and tights and texted Mo—the only other person she knew who loved dance as much.

JahMeeLah: *can't believe how many leos I have. Six so far . . . that fit.* 😬

Mo'Betta: *no more cakes?* 😂

JahMeeLah: 😕

The stupid nickname made her smile. Even if it hadn't been funny at the time she got it.

After her first year in dance she'd grown three inches, and by the time classes started in August every single leo rode up her butt. It was so embarrassing. Tai had called her "Cakes" for a week. No way she was letting that happen this year.

Mo'Betta: *what r u doing for the jazz part of the TAG audition?* ••)

Mila sat on her bed with a thump. She'd barely given the new talented and gifted program a thought. Track had been the first time she'd tried out for anything. But it wasn't like anybody got cut. Everybody got at least one event. She assumed TAG would be the same. Wouldn't they all get placed somewhere just for trying out?

Now Mo's text made her doubt that. And she couldn't ask any questions because her dad had been on the committee that reviewed the program and recommended it to the school board. Nobody believed that Mila didn't know every single detail. Luckily Mo talked on, so she wouldn't have to admit how little she knew.

Mo'Betta: *its gotta be 45 seconds long. Imma do a part from Sara Strut? member dat?* 😬

JahMeeLah: *yessss!* 😂 😐

Sara Strut was their first jazz dance with La May. Her and Mo had a featured role dancing in front of the other girls for two whole eight counts. If you blinked or looked down at your program, you missed it. Still, Tai had been so mad that she hadn't been featured that she fussed about it a whole month after the recital was over.

Mo'Betta: *I already picked out the part I want do*

JahMeeLah: 🙂 *u way ahead of me. For real I haven't thought about it. . . . guess I better*

Mo'Betta: *probz should. Imma ask Noelle if I can practice it after class. If she say yes stay after w/me. We can help each other get ready*

JahMeeLah: *kk*

A text from Tai flashed on the screen. Instantly Mila felt guilty for enjoying the chat with Mo so much. Tai texted with Mo and Sheeda without her all the time, usually because Mila didn't answer her phone fast enough. Still, they were all friends. How come it felt so wrong now?

She promised Mo she'd hit her up if they ended up in center court and switched to Tai.

DatGirlTai: *furreal if Rollie mentions TAG one more time I'mma merc him*

JahMeeLah: *yeah sure ya will* 😤 *He pretty hyped huh?*

DatGirlTai: *try super hyped & thas fine but anytime I'm not hyped back he act like I'm the one wrong. TAG ain't gonna be no different than Girls Run. Whus to be excited about?* 😒

Finding things to argue about was Tai's job. She did it good enough for the both of them. So Mila knew not to say what was really on her mind—that even if TAG was like other after-school programs, what was wrong with that? It was better than sitting around or walking the streets.

JahMeeLah: *it'll be something different to do though. I'm not mad at that*

DatGirlTai: *Of course u not. Everybody know ur father would make u try out no matter what. Gotta keep her highness outta trouble.* 😄 *don't even get mad cuz I'm joking!*

JahMeeLah: *u not but it's w/e* 😛

DatGirlTai: *lolz*

Stuff with Tai had a way of starting out as a joke but not ending there, so Mila asked about Roland.

JahMeeLah: *so R u and Roland official?* 👀

DatGirlTai: *I wish. He so slow. Like boy what r u waiting for?!*

JahMeeLah: *will be weird to see yall as a couple*

DatGirlTai: *Why?* 😠

JahMeeLah: *jus b/c we've known him 4eva*

DatGirlTai: *oh. I guess*

For a few minutes there was nothing. Mila figured

the conversation was over since Tai couldn't ask her to come hang out. It was Wednesday. Ms. Sophia worked late Wednesday night and slept most of the day. So no company allowed. She was lost in the rhythm of sorting the leos into two piles—giveaway and throw away—when Tai came back minutes later.

DatGirlTai: *Hey sorry. Rollie just hit me up. they balling later. Let's hit center court and hook up wit em*

Mila read the message again like putting the words in a different order might make them mean something else.

Center court.

Rollie.

Hook up.

Nope. They still meant having to see Roland.

Ugh. Talking about him was one thing. Tai was always talking about him. So there was no avoiding that. Seeing him was another. She wasn't ready. But she wasn't about to tell Tai that. It was complicated.

She hadn't talked to any of her friends over the summer. Then one day she'd gone to the court, down from Aunt Jacqs' house, and seen Roland—never Rollie to her. *Rollie* sounded like a short, fat bald guy that did the announcements at church on Sunday.

It had been so weird seeing somebody from the Cove in the Woods. But there Roland had been, standing on the sidelines of the basketball court with another guy who turned out to be his cousin, Michael. He'd looked up, squinted in her direction, then sauntered over.

Without Tai there grinning in his face and interrupting the conversation, they'd ended up talking for a long time about life in the burbs and going into the eighth grade. Then she'd run into him again, at the Garret Carnival, and they'd talked until Cinny and her friends had gotten off the devil's whirl. After that he texted her a few times. Mostly to talk about what it was really like in the Woods because he was thinking of staying with his cousin the next summer.

He seemed different outside of their neighborhood. Until he mentioned TAG she didn't know that he played the drums, was auditioning, and was thinking of starting a go-go band. Roland rarely said more than he had to. Sometimes he was quiet to the point of being antisocial. When he did talk, it was always in the most simple sentences. It pleased her that they'd talked so much and so easily without the rest of the crew around.

Then one day Cinny saw her squirreled away texting him and teased her about having a boyfriend.

After that she stopped answering his text messages. She didn't want him thinking she was pushing up on him. He was Tai's crush.

Eventually his messages stopped. She had put it out of her mind, until now.

DatGirlTai: *????? hello u down? Don't flake on me. We only have a few weeks left to kick it before school starts.* 🙏

Reluctantly Mila agreed to go.

Remembering her chats with Roland made her tingly with anxiety. She would tell Tai all about it when she had time to explain the whole thing. She prayed he wouldn't say anything until she could.

As soon as they rounded the corner, Tai squealed. Mila's head swiveled. She didn't know whether to duck or run. Was it a gun? A fight? She looked up in time to see that it was only Roland, Simp, and a guy she didn't recognize in front of the rec. Tai pulled her by the wrist across the street toward them.

Mila grasped at her shirt as it slid down her shoulder showing what little boobage she had. "Dang, Tai." She tried to hold it up and keep her balance, but Tai was on a mission.

Roland bounced a basketball, slow and easy,

dribbling it in between his legs while Simp pointed at the rec, saying something to the new guy. Tai placed herself in front of them. "Hey, y'all." Her smile reached her eyes, making them crinkle.

Mila snatched her bra strap up, hoping the boys hadn't noticed, before adding herself to the small semicircle. Her eyes darted away from Roland. She fixed them on Simp.

"What up, Tai-Tai?" Simp said. He licked his lips and leered at her, showing off a single platinum cap on his front tooth. His thick mane of dreads, pulled back with a single black band, reached his shoulders. It made him look like somebody from *The Lion King*.

Never one to pretend when she wasn't feeling somebody, Tai frowned. "Nothing, Simp. And you know I hate being called 'Tai-Tai.'" She dug in her shorts pocket and pulled out a tube of lip balm. "You need this?"

The new guy managed to keep a straight face. Roland looked on with bored amusement.

Simp frowned down at the lip balm. "Why?"

Tai shrugged. "Oh you was licking your lips so . . . "

She put it back, the bust obvious to everybody but Simp.

Mila caught Roland looking at her. There was a smirk at the corner of his mouth. Mila's eyes fled back to Tai. She was smiling so fiercely her face looked like it was going to crack.

"Y'all ready go ball?" Tai asked. Her fingers combed through the long, slinky side of her hair.

Roland's mouth twisted slightly like "what you think?" Then he looked right at Mila. "Hey, Bean." He dribbled the ball hard, once, making it bounce into his hand. He held it under his arm. "I thought maybe you was gone for good like your sister."

She cleared the squeak out of her throat. "Nope. Back on the block."

He lifted his chin, nodding in approval. For a second, their eyes locked. Once again, Mila prayed, silently but hard, that their summer chats weren't worth bringing up.

The word *secret* whispered in her mind and made her pits sweat.

He bounced the ball, again—*ping, ping,* hold. *Ping, ping,* hold. The longer he did it, the more relieved Mila was. He'd said all he was going to say. She breathed, calm, happy when Tai—tired of the conversation leaking away from her—changed the subject.

"So who's this?" She gave the new guy a good long look from head to toe.

Without being as brazen, Mila scoped him out herself.

He was brown skinned with big brown eyes and fifteen rows of braids going straight back. She was eye to eye with him. So he had to be about five foot five.

"I'm Chris," the guy said with an easy nod.

Tai played hostess. "I'm Metai and this is . . ."

"I'm Jamila, but you can call me Mila." She raised her eyebrow at Tai.

Of course Tai was unable to let it go without saying something smart.

"Mila love calling people by their government name." Tai rolled her eyes then raised a playful eyebrow. "I hope you don't have a nickname, Chris. If you do she won't be calling you by it."

Only Simp brayed in appreciation at Tai's sarcasm. He was forever on a quest for her approval.

"People who go back with her call her 'Bean,' though," Roland said. "We still allowed to call you that?"

Mila's heart quick-stepped across her chest. She felt like she knew him better now. She didn't want to say no and seem petty. But she wasn't about to let some stranger call her "Bean."

"I mean, I really wish people would just call me Mila. I outgrew Bean a minute ago." She plastered a polite smile on her face, hoping he understood.

Tai pursed her lips—either mad about being corrected or because the attention wasn't solely on her. Before she could say anything, Roland deaded the conversation.

"Cool. All right . . . Mila then," he said.

Tai jumped in the second it grew quiet. "So, Chris, like, where are you from that you still rocking straight backs, for real?"

Simp's dreads shook as he burst into a fit of laughter. Chris smirked at Tai like she was funny but not funny enough to make him laugh.

"Virginia" was his only answer.

"Ay, yo, Chris is here to try out for TAG." Roland looked at Mila. "He auditioning for Vocal Arts."

Tai pouted in Roland's general direction. "I be so glad when auditions over."

"I thought you was excited to try out for dance," Roland said. He looked genuinely confused.

Mila was, too. Tai always acted like she hated dance.

She almost said it. But the realization that Tai had obviously told Roland something different hushed her. It relieved her, too. If Roland and Tai had talked so much, the little bit she had talked to him wouldn't matter.

"I mean I'mma at least try out," Tai said sheepishly, then she raised her eyebrow high. "As long as it ain't just all ballet. Ain't nobody trying to be a bun head."

Mila took the dig graciously. Tai took her being good at ballet personally. At first it hurt her feelings when everybody but Tai would compliment her on a good class. Now the jabs about ballet being boring or played out was noise—just one more thing her and Tai didn't agree on. She steered the conversation back to the new guy. "So which part of the vocal program you trying out for? Singing? Songwriting or . . ."

"Lyrical flow," Chris answered, seeming to know what she was reaching for. He smiled like he was apologizing for having to remember for her.

Mila returned the smile. He was a little cute, straight-back cornrows and all.

Roland bounced the ball then feigned taking a shot. "Man, I don't know why they don't just call it rap. They trying too hard with some lyrical flow."

He and Chris shared the same choppy laugh. Every

boy Mila knew did it. There was no mistaking they were clowning something when they laughed that way. JJ laughed like that all the time when he was poking fun at something she or Jeremy said. Even Jeremy was starting to do it sometimes. She had thought it was only a Cove thing.

"True dat," Chris said. "I can definitely spit a little bit. . . ."

"You mean flow lyrically?" Roland said, making them both laugh hard, for real this time. They knocked knuckles.

Simp gritted on Chris, his lip arched in a snarl like the conversation was boring him. Mila felt a little bad for him. Roland and Chris were already talking like they'd known each other for a while. She could see how Simp felt left out.

"Righ' righ'," Chris said. "Well, I been singing since—"

"If you can already sing, what you need some program for?" Simp asked, lip pooched in disgust.

"Simp just salty 'cause he can't try out. He not in eighth grade yet," Tai said, spreading the boy's business without thought.

Simp's eyes went to the ground. He sat back in the

cut, silent the rest of the conversation.

"I don't need no program to sing," Chris said more to the group than directly at Simp. "TAG got a songwriting track. Most programs don't. And I'm trying tighten my writing game." He smashed his fist lightly into his hands, growing animated. "Songwriters make bank, for real. So I'm doing the vocal program with a concentration in songwriting."

Mila had never heard anybody lay out where they were going "in the future." She hadn't thought about TAG like that at all.

"You saying you moved from Virginia just for this?" Tai asked. She stared wide-eyed like Chris had landed from a spaceship and had two heads.

He gazed at her defiantly. "Yeah, me and my sister."

"Who moves to another state not even knowing if they gonna get into the program?" Tai looked around the circle, waiting on somebody to jump in and cosign her interrogation. Simp's mouth was set like he was determined not to answer anything that had to do with Chris.

Instead of answering Tai, Chris turned his back slightly to her and Simp and talked mainly to Roland. "My mother figured we'd have a better chance of getting in since it's a brand-new program."

"'Cause y'all all that?" Tai said, refusing to be iced out of the conversation.

Chris glanced over his shoulder at her. "I ain't bragging or nothing. It's just fact, I been singing since I was, like, three years old."

"I don't mean no harm but that seem crazy to me," Tai said. But the hard edge in her voice was gone. She wasn't going to get a rise out of Chris no matter how hard she tried.

"Don't knock the man's game," Roland said, adding insult to injury.

"Ain't nobody knocking his game," she muttered, crossing her arms. But that was it. She kept her usual sarcasm locked away.

Mila was fascinated. Guys were usually nice to Tai and flirty with her while Mila sat on the sideline feeling invisible. And Chris wasn't mean about it. He was time enough for Tai and her questions. If him and Roland ever got close enough, maybe Roland would warn Chris that Tai was likely keeping score of every little law he broke. Though Chris didn't seem like the type of person who would care. She decided right then she liked him. Even more as he went on, talking, unaware of the daggers Tai was shooting at him.

"These programs be wanting a good mix of people who already got 'it' and a few they can help be better at what they do. At least that's how the one where I used to live worked. But they always got a waiting list. So—" He shrugged. Without Tai's interruptions and all the attention finally on him, he seemed uncomfortable for the first time. "Anyway. But good luck to whoever trying out." He put his fist out. Roland knocked it. "All right, Rollie, man. Thanks for showing my sister where the rec was. See you on the court."

He walked off without saying boo to Simp.

Tai's head whipped from Roland to Chris's disappearing figure.

Roland stage-whispered, "He kind of read you, Tai."

Mila held her breath waiting for the explosion.

"Shut up, Rollie," Tai said without an ounce of anger. Her eyes narrowed. "He got a sister, huh?"

"Yeah. They twins," Simp offered, happy to be back in the conversation. "She take dance. Probably in y'all class."

Tai's eyes lit up. "Fresh meat."

"Shoot, if she anything like him she can handle you," Roland said.

"Whatever," Tai said. But there was no fire in her voice. She elbowed Roland then stepped closer to him until her boob brushed his arm.

Mila's thoughts turned to Chris. He was a twin. That was cool. She couldn't remember the last time somebody their age had moved into the hood. That had to be a good sign. Maybe the Cove was changing some.

Against her will, hope built in her chest.

CHAPTER
6

The new dude was lucky Tai had been in a good mood. She had come real close to busting him out a few times. Especially when he turned his back on her.

The only reason she didn't say anything—Rollie. Not that Rollie had some kind of control over her or anything. Hmph, he wished. But no, it wasn't that. At least not totally. She was trying to respect that him and Rollie was vibing. Over TAG, of course. And if she had said how she really felt—that all this fuss over TAG was like trying to put air back into a burst balloon, a waste of time—it might have made Rollie mad. So she had chilled.

Plus, once he mentioned he had a sister, she knew she'd have a chance for some get back. Tai couldn't wait to see her and give her a little Cove welcome. She snickered 'cause the last thing she felt, right now, was welcoming. Sometimes dance put her in a straight-up bad mood.

She had a love-hate relationship with it.

She loved jazz-hated ballet. Loved getting out of the house for a few hours-hated how long class lasted sometimes, especially toward the end of ballet when her knees and back were sore from trying to hold a position that made her look like a demented pretzel. Seriously, who could stand with their feet up against each other but facing opposite directions? That didn't even sound right.

She pulled on a pair of pink tights then sucked her teeth. She had forgotten to take off her underwear. She always did and Noelle always got all extra lecturing about a dancer's proper uniform. It was just hair and a pair of drawls. Who cared? Still, she took off the underwear with unnecessary force.

Once in class, she was thankful she had remembered. Everyone was dressed properly, little clones following every direction Noelle uttered. Even the new girl. How'd she already know the rules? Tai hated her on sight.

She was brown skinned like an almond. Her hair was straight and shiny in a tight, high bun. It sat on top of her head, thick and fat like someone had wrapped the hair around a donut. She was even taller than Bean and just as skinny. A ballerina's body. Tai swallowed the thought bitterly, for once falling out of love with her own curves and thickity goodness.

New girl's round, brown eyes flickered up, watching them all stream in. Tai watched her watching them.

Their chatter grew as the girls who hadn't seen Bean welcomed her back. People were really acting like it was a big deal that she'd been gone a minute.

Mo cawed about her brother being busted coming in late through the window. It didn't surprise Tai. Lenny was dumb as dirt. Fifteen and still didn't know how to sneak.

CoCo asked Bean had she heard about the fire in fourth court. Tai had already told her but Bean listened politely. She clucked a few words of sympathy in the right places, all so she wouldn't hurt CoCo's feelings by admitting, "Oh yeah, I heard." It made Tai mad all over again about Bean's request to be called by her real name. She just didn't get it.

If she wanted everybody else to call her "Mila," cool. But they were best friends. If anybody should get a pass and be able to call her "Bean" or whatever she wanted, wasn't it her? She flicked her flip-flop off. It flew across the room. Mo gave the flip-flop and Tai one of her looks. Bean only glanced at it curiously.

Tai knew it was childish. She didn't care. She was bored with their conversation. She looked at Chris's sister on the edge of the group. It was exactly where Tai planned to keep her if she could help it. She waited, patiently, until new girl looked her way. When she did, Tai raised her eyebrow to make sure the new girl knew she was being watched back. The two shiny brown marbles flicked away, looking down at the stretch bands in her hand.

Exactly, just so you know, Tai thought.

She looked for a resemblance to the country-cute boy with the curly lashes and half dimples she'd met days before. They didn't look anything alike. That was disappointing. She had thought they'd be identical. They barely looked related, much less like twins. She wasn't even all that cute, but Cove dudes would think so just because she was new. Maybe even Rollie.

Tai stared, fiery jealousy in her chest as the girl

followed behind Noelle, with soft, elegant steps, placing the bands where the teacher told her to. Another teacher's pet.

Bean was bad enough with her "Mademoiselle this" and "Mademoiselle that" in a quiet voice like she was calling on God. Every time she did it, Tai sucked her teeth and snapped, "You mean *Miss* Noelle?" but she hadn't been able to break her out of it. Bean worshipped their teacher.

She jumped back into the conversation when Sheeda started a story about visiting her cousins on some farm next summer. Nobody wanted to hear nothing about no farm. "So who wanna hear what Rollie texted me the other day?" she asked, cutting Sheeda off.

The girls immediately quieted down. Every pair of eyes was on her. The attention made her giddy. None of them had boyfriends yet. The race to be the first had been on unofficially since last year. Tai had no worries she'd come out the winner. If Rollie would move a little faster, she'd win before school started.

She bragged about how Rollie had texted her "what's up?" She paused in all the right places, leaving areas blank so the girls would believe there was more to his text than it was.

"Rollie cute but he weird," Sheeda said. She pulled her Senegalese twists back, not bothering to bun the heavy hair. "He too quiet. It seem like he just sitting back watching what everybody do."

Tai rolled her eyes. "It ain't like he can get a word in when you start yapping, Sheeda."

Bean squinted a crinkle-eyed reprimand. She touched Sheeda's shoulder. "I think he just used to being by his self. It's just him and his grandmother and mother when he's home."

"I guess," Sheeda said slowly.

"Whatever," Tai said, before Sheeda could blurt out more nonsense. "Once I get with Rollie, y'all can fight over the dudes left. Like Simp." She raised her eyebrow at Bean. "Lenny." Then Mo. "And JJ."

Mo folded her arms and glared at Tai. "No shade to JJ but how you figure me and Bean supposed to get with each other's brothers? You didn't hardly name anybody."

"I know, right." Sheeda scowled in thought. "And it's plenty other dudes in the Cove. Why you only name those three?"

"Look, those are the cute and cute-ish ones," Tai said, sounding like a disappointed teacher.

Bean's eyes bucked wide. "You think Simp is cute?"

It set everybody off laughing.

"I said cute-ish," Tai said, her face hot with embarrassment. She threw Bean a look. Whose side was she on?

"Wow! If Simp ever heard you thought he was cute-ish, that would make his life," Mo said, cawing.

"Definitely." Sheeda patted Tai's leg gently. "But you know your secret safe with us."

Tai raised her voice over their teasing. "Oh my God. I was just trying name dudes, like, our age. It's not my fault Rollie the best of the bunch."

"Who died and made you the matchmaker?" Mo asked with open disgust. She snatched a ballet slipper and snapped it on her foot.

"Look I don't care who y'all get with, long as you know Rollie mine," Tai said.

"Like, who wouldn't?" Mo asked. "You been on his tip since fifth grade." She put on the other ballet slipper, walked off, and took her place in the first row. The other girls followed suit.

Tai stayed sitting on the floor, taking her time getting her slippers on. She wasn't about to shadow Mo. Her heart pounded angrily at being left behind. She thought about faking cramps and leaving class. She wasn't really in the mood anymore, then Noelle clapped her hands twice. "Girls . . . *allons.*"

The girls clapped back once. Class had started.

Tai reluctantly joined the fray, silently throwing darts at Mo's back.

Chris's sister stayed in place, beside Noelle, her eyes wandering just above their heads.

Bean stood perfectly erect in the center of the front row. Her feet were turned out, in first position, arms at her sides ready to bust into first on demand. Chandra, Shayla, and Monique stood in the same line, waiting.

Bean and the new girl had the same long torso and legs that seemed to go on forever. "A dancer's body." At least that's what Tai had overheard Noelle tell Bean about her shape once. Tai had almost pointed out that the dancers on videos and TV had thick, strong legs like her, but Noelle had said it low like it was meant only for Bean—Tai didn't want them to know she was being nosy.

The four girls in the second row imitated the first row. Their backs weren't as straight. Their hips not as turned out, but Tai knew they were working hard to get moved up. Once they'd realized the rows were based on skill. They all wanted to be top dog. Tai hated how much she cared.

Sheeda and CoCo were in her row. She glanced over at them. CoCo was in the right position (mostly) but Sheeda was standing relaxed waiting for Mademoiselle to demand the position. Tai stood up a little straighter, but refused to put her feet and arms in position. It looked crazy doing that before class officially started.

Noelle waited patiently, hands clasped until everyone was quiet. She was tall and thin and seemed to sprout from the floor like a weed from the ground. Until Noelle, Tai had never seen a Black French person. Even now it was weird hearing a musical accent come out of someone that looked like her. She was from Canada, but every time Noelle opened her mouth, visions of the Eiffel Tower filled Tai's head.

Once she could hear a pin drop, Noelle beamed at them. "Welcome back. I must say I'm surprised some of you returned." She winked at Tai, making the other girls laugh quietly. Tai gave her that one. She couldn't be annoyed because it was true—she was always nearly one foot out the door.

"I just came back for the jazz," Tai called out, to show she could joke, too.

"I believe you," Noelle said with a knowing laugh. "Before I introduce you to our new student, I just want to remind you, one more time, about TAG auditions. For those of you auditioning, please come prepared. Stretch, practice, and get dance into your heads. This will be new and challenging."

As Tai expected, Mo's hand shot up. "Mademoiselle, are they making cuts or are the auditions for show?"

"For show?" Noelle's eyebrows furrowed. She reverted to French, something she did when she was trying to understand how to explain something. "*Mais non*. There will be cuts."

A disappointed sigh exploded in the studio. Tai couldn't tell if it was Mo, Bean, or somebody else.

Sheeda piped in without raising her hand. "Like, does your vote count more than the other judges, though?"

"Again, *non*. I am only one vote. It's why I'm asking you to bring what you girls call your 'A game.'" Noelle pointed to a banner above the mirror—*If you love it, work for it. Si vous l'aimez, se travailler pour elle.* "Remember the La Maison philosophy. Yes?" Enough girls chorused back to satisfy her. "Good. And remember there are other disciplines in the new program—art, music, and drama. Do not close your minds to something new."

Sheeda nudged Tai. "We should try out for drama."

Tai scrunched her nose. "Just 'cause you too scared to try out for dance don't mean I am."

"I'm not scared. Just realistic." Sheeda sniffed. "Hello, we still in the third row."

Like Tai needed the reminder. She waved at Sheeda to hush, but the seed of doubt had been planted.

Noelle got so extra during ballet, always trying to force Tai's body to do stuff it just couldn't do. It was like she couldn't see Tai was doing her best. Now here came Sheeda pointing out they were the slow learners.

She tuned back in as Noelle was finishing up.

"If anyone wants to use the dance studio to rehearse their audition piece, please just let me know. I will make sure you have any access you need. Yes?" She went on like anyone had answered. "So, everyone, this is Christol." Her arm wrapped around the new girl's shoulders. She beamed as the girls said hello in unison. "*Merci*. She's new to class and the Cove. I expect you to embrace her. She is now part of the La Maison family." With her accent it came out "fah-me." "Christol please tell us a little bit about yourself." She took a step back, giving Christol the spotlight.

Christol looked like she might run out the door. Her

voice was quiet when she finally said, "My name is Christol Mason." She cleared her throat and spoke up.

"I just moved here from Richmond. I'm going into the eighth grade." She stood up straighter and more confident. "I've been taking dance since I was five years old. Ballet, tap, and jazz. We moved here so I could audition for the new magnet program." A look passed between her and Noelle. It made Noelle smile proudly and seemed to comfort Christol. "I used to dance competitively, for a few years." She looked over at Noelle, unsure again. Tai caught the instructor's tiny head nod and rolled her eyes. Like, girl, spit it out.

Christol took a breath, "I'vetakenfirstinmylyrical-andjazzcategorytentimes." With that out, she talked normally again. "I'm taking a break from competing, so I can focus on technique. One day I want to get into a good dance school."

The girls in the first two rows murmured like she'd just announced she could fly. Mo glanced back at Tai, in the mirror, grinning. She was competitive and probably loving this. But it made Tai anxious. Christol had more experience than all of them. The last thing she needed was somebody else automatically moved up to the first row.

Noelle stepped back beside Christol.

"Thank you, Christol," she said, pronouncing it, "Chris-Tall." "If you don't mind, please go stand in line next to Metai . . . Metai, raise your hand." She gently pushed Christol toward Tai's barely raised hand. "You're new to our warm-ups and routine. This will give me a chance to see where you should be placed."

Nerves crawled all over Tai like ants. If Christol was any good, she would look ridiculous next to her. She took a deep breath.

In her head, Tai knew the key was to transition from one position to the other smoothly, arms gracefully arcing from empty beach ball to left G—the terms Noelle had introduced them to before moving to the true ballet terms for first and fourth positions. In real life, Tai had a hard time catching the awkward rhythm.

Noelle turned the music on and walked between the rows calling out positions in a singsongy melody that floated above the music instead of with it. Tai watched, in the mirror, as Bean moved in time without any thought. She willed her body to do the same. Her face was a mask of concentration as she tried to ride the beat.

"And first position . . . second . . . third and fourth," Noelle's voice called.

She stopped in front of Bean. Her eyes were everywhere at once. She nodded at some girls. Others she fixed with a head shake or worse, pursed lips, as she called, "First, now second, and third and fourth." Satisfied with Bean's performance, she walked on. "First now fifth and back to fourth. Third now second and back to first."

The closer Noelle got, the more flustered Tai became. She was a beat behind and when her feet cooperated, her arms wouldn't. Tai jerked them to the right. The correction caught Noelle's attention. Tai gritted her teeth as Noelle reached her in three soft but firm steps, placed her arms high and tight, the right way, then moved on.

Before she had a chance to breathe their teacher was back, this time in front of Christol. From the corner of her eye, Tai saw Christol moving effortlessly from one position to the next. It made her face burn with angry frustration.

Tai looked at herself in the mirror, and directed her legs and arms the right way. She couldn't worry about the new girl right now.

Class had just gotten real. It was time to grind.

CHAPTER
7

Mila's first thought when her eyes popped open the next morning—*I like Christol*. The second thought was, When had her arms and legs been replaced by burning hot rubber bands? Her muscles were so sore, even wiggling her fingers made her biceps pop in protest. Every burst of pain reminded her how graceful Christol had been. She probably wasn't in pain today.

When Christol seemed afraid to admit how long she'd been dancing, that's when Mila knew she liked her. If Christol didn't know the rest of them had only danced for two short years at first, she did after the class was over. But she'd still touched Mila on the shoulder as they were leaving, and complimented her. "Your leaps were pretty."

The four words made Mila float on air. It also made her feel bad. Mo, Sheeda, and CoCo had said the same thing to her before a few times, but hearing it from Christol made Mila believe it more. She knew that was kind of wrong. But somebody who had never seen her dance before complimenting her made Mila feel like a real dancer. She was even getting excited about TAG.

Excited was probably too strong a word. The twins talked about TAG like it was passage to a different world where kids already had their future on lock. Mila was curious. Would TAG be that way? Or was Tai right that it would be like a lot of other after-school programs, here for a year or two then gone?

She'd attempted to ask Christol what it was like to do dance competitions, but Tai had summoned her, telling her to hurry up. And like a sheep Mila had bit back her question and followed. She walked away embarrassed, promising herself to stop doing everything the way she'd always done it. It's why she had to talk to her dad. If she didn't, nothing would ever change and it would be her own fault.

She pushed herself out of bed. Sore arms and legs or not, there was a Phillips Saturday routine to maintain. She reported to the living room as her dad directed what chores had to be done and went over the rest of the day's schedule. If Mila was okay with it, he and the boys would be going to Padonia, a park known for having extra-competitive pickup games.

It would leave Mila an entire day to chill in a quiet house, maybe even watch the big TV. For that kind of peace, she would have volunteered to do the boys' chores for them if it got them out of the house faster. She kept that to herself.

Once her dad was confident she wouldn't wither away while they were gone, he laced her with a few dollars for whatever the day brought.

Music blared through the house to help them get through the work—bathroom duty for her, kitchen cleanup for JJ, and vacuuming for Jeremy, about the only job he could do where you couldn't tell if it was done wrong or not. Her dad wandered from room to room making sure the chores were being done to his expectations. With the boys downstairs and the music loud enough to cover her, the next time he walked by the bathroom she called out, "Daddy, can I talk to you real quick?"

He pivoted like a soldier. "Yup. Or you can talk to me real slow if you want."

They both laughed at the lame joke.

Her dad posted himself in the doorway of the small bathroom. Mila sat on the edge of the tub and beckoned him in closer. He leaned against the sink, careful not to put all his weight on it. Thanks to her brothers, stuff in their row house broke in the dumbest ways. Most times their dad fixed it himself instead of calling the maintenance office. The sink was the latest in a long line of don't ask/don't tell fixes after JJ had sat on it, pulling the thing out of the wall.

His eyes glittered the way they always did when he was really listening.

Mila looked past him. She didn't want Jeremy to walk up on her talking about this. Not after she'd made a promise. The coast was clear, but she still lowered her voice.

"Would you ever let me move to Aunt Jacqs'?"

Just saying it made her anxious. But summer would be fall soon and life would get back to normal, and life as normal included hanging over Tai's. The thought brought back hot, shameful memories of Tai's father touching her. By mistake? It could have been.

It hadn't felt like it.

If it had been a mistake, how come Tai's eyes had widened then narrowed as she scowled at Mr. Bryant afterward? How come the next time Tai invited her over and Mila asked, "Is your father going to be home?" Tai got loud, almost like she was mad that Mila had brought him up. She reprimanded Mila like she was a bad child. "Bean, you know how ignorant he can be. Ignore him like I do."

Mila had tried. She really had. It hadn't worked. She couldn't go over to Tai's and act like nothing had happened. But she couldn't hide not going, either.

Her dad folded his arms and kicked one foot over the other. He cracked himself up again. "Is this a real question or you just asking to have options to escape the general Phillips crazy?"

Mila smiled weakly through her churning stomach. "I wouldn't mind living with Aunt Jacqs. I had fun this summer."

"I have no doubt you did. But being there a few weeks and living there is different." He pushed the lid down on the commode and sat. "Why would I send you to Aunt Jacqi's, babe?"

Mila instantly regretted asking. Her brain froze as

she tried to come up with an answer he'd believe. Their mother was a drug addict who was no longer welcome in the house until she was clean. She knew it. And they knew it. So when he asked you something in that quiet, probing voice, playtime was over. She wasn't ready for the conversation because it wasn't like she could tell him the real reason—that she didn't want to live across the street from Mr. Bryant anymore if she didn't have to.

"Well, you sent Cinny for high school," she said, holding on to the only true answer she had.

"I did," he agreed. His eyebrows furrowed and unfurrowed like he was trying to decide which emotion to show. They ended up high and straight—a bad attempt at hiding that she'd caught him off his game. "Because I sent Cinny, you just figured I'd send you to live with Aunt Jacqs, too?" He asked the question slow and carefully. Mila wasn't sure whether it was to make sure she understood it or so he understood it himself. "Just like that?"

With "yes" caught in her throat, Mila could only nod. Her confidence faded as the certainty in his voice grew.

"There's no way you'd know this, but sending Jacinta away was one of the hardest decisions I ever made." He tapped her wrist softly, keeping beat to the conversation. "It was the right thing for her. But it's my job to raise you and your brothers. I'm not going to keep shipping y'all off." He touched her chin, swiveling her face upward. "Cinny was getting too close to things in the streets that could have sucked her in. You're different—"

He paused. If there were things in the Cove sucking her in, now was the time to tell him. Tell him and he'd fix it because that's what her dad did. His light brown eyes questioned and his fingers pressed softly into her flesh, encouraging her to be truthful.

She opened her mouth, breathed in—unsure what was going to come out—then nodded. Telling the truth wasn't an option.

His wide grin—assuming they were on the same page again—hurt her. They weren't even in the same book, much less on the same page. She bit the inside of her lip to stop it from trembling as he ticked off what made her so special.

"You're not afraid of life outside of the Cove, Jamila. You like school, you dance, and you're curious about the world. Jacinta wasn't. The Cove was her world and getting her to leave wasn't easy." That was an understatement. Cinny hated life in the Woods at first. His face darkened at the memory. "But you have TAG to look forward to. If you went to Aunt Jacqs', you'd miss out on that opportunity. Know what else?" He swung playfully at one of the micro braids that slithered around her shoulders. "I miss Cinny too much. I did what I had to do for her. But sending her to live with Jacqi made me realize that my kids' place is definitely here with me. Good or bad. So I'm gonna do my best by you and your brothers." His smile was crooked. "How am I doing so far?"

Mila wanted to be done with the conversation. Before the smile on her face could slide away, she tipped her hand side to side. Her dad's laugh boomed inside the small space. He'd shot down the only plan she had for getting away from Mr. Bryant. The room felt like it was spinning.

"Just so-so huh? Ouch." He pecked her forehead with his lips. "I'll try and do better in the future, baby girl."

He thundered down the stairs, leaving Mila reeling.

"Boys, be ready when I get back from the store," he boomed over the music.

Once the front door slammed, Mila squeezed her eyes tight. She was relieved and frustrated at the same time. Relieved that she hadn't had to tell him what happened that day in Tai's yard. Frustrated that her dad was suddenly Mr. Answer Right Away.

Seriously, any other time they asked him anything, he had to "sleep on it."

When JJ wanted to quit the Cougars basketball team, he'd slept on that for two days before telling JJ that quitting mid-season wasn't an option. When Mila asked could she take Mandarin instead of Spanish, he'd thought it over nearly a week before deciding it made no sense for her to learn a language she'd never use versus one she could use with one out of every four of her neighbors.

What happened to sleeping on it? It wasn't fair.

Didn't her dad know there was stuff in the Cove that could pull her in, too?

Didn't he know he couldn't protect her from everything?

The realization filled her with gloomy despair.

With one long leg she reached out and nudged the bathroom door shut so her brothers wouldn't see the tears running down her face. She laid her forehead on her knees and breathed through the brick on her chest, doing her best to muffle the sobs.

CHAPTER
8

"The TAG countdown is real out here in these streets," Rollie's voice said from Tai's laptop.

They'd been on Skyvo chatting for the last thirty minutes and it was the first time he'd mentioned TAG. That was progress as far as she was concerned. She balanced the laptop on her knees, her back against her bed. Luckily she'd gotten up early and wasn't looking scary when his chat call came through. Score a point for Nona and her mandatory breakfasts.

Thanks to all the overtime she worked, breakfast was the only meal she and Tai were guaranteed to share. Even when her father was staying with them, it was exclusively her and Nona's time since he acted like rising before ten would literally kill him.

"You're so daggone pressed," Tai said, hoping it came out as a joke like she'd meant it.

Rollie lectured her. "Naw, it's called ambition. *Pressed* is when you open for something you might not get."

"Shoot, you might not get this," she said. She was almost gentle as she continued. "Anybody can get cut, Rollie. It's an audition."

A flicker of doubt crossed his face, then his chill returned. "I know. But I don't plan on being one of 'em." He turned it on her. "You should be the one nervous. I heard the dance joint is the hardest thing to get into."

There was a part of Tai that didn't care. There had been TAGs before. Girls Run. Sparking Art. Team Tennis Frenzy. And Urban Vogue, a modeling program. She had just known she was going to be America's Next Top Model until the coordinator called her "stumpy." It hurt her feelings enough to send her home crying. Nona had come back, fire in her eyes, and laid Ms. Jordana out. Tai never returned. A few months later Ms. Jordana stopped showing up and the program disappeared like sand in the wind.

She didn't get why anybody thought TAG was going to be any different than the other stuff that came in barrels blazing to help keep kids off the street. It would be hot for a while then go away or change, just like how the rec used to be open every day for a few hours and now it was only open two days a week. Whenever people called themselves making the Cove better, it was all talk. It was like she was the only one who felt that way, though.

She dared to be honest with Rollie.

"All the papers they gave us about dance seem like it's talking about ballet anyway." Everything was always about ballet. "If it's only about stupid positions in French and boring piano music, they can miss me with that."

"Yeah, well, my cousin Mike be with the Players and they helping put the program together," Rollie said, unbothered by her answer. "He gave me some scoop—said it's already, like, eighty applications in for the dance part."

Eighty? Sounded like they had told the whole world about these auditions. She sucked her lips in then forced her shoulders to shrug. "I guess we just got wait and see."

Her grandmother's voice nagged faintly in the distance, saving her.

"Ay, I gotta go." She carried the laptop to the desk. "We gonna chill later with Bean at center court?"

"You mean Mila?" he corrected sternly then laughed.

She loved how cute he looked when he laughed. But she rolled her eyes at him. "Whatever. Sometimes I remember and sometimes I don't." It was the most honest she'd ever been about the whole thing. "So you coming or naw?"

Maybe she was crazy but it felt like she was starting to wrap him around her finger, a tiny bit at least.

"Yeah, we be there," he said.

Tai felt like pumping her fist in victory.

Wait. Had he said "we"? Ugh.

She started to tell him to leave Simp home, but Nona's voice grew closer. She was in the hallway and Tai didn't want her to come in and get loud about what was she doing blah-blah.

"All right, later," she said, logging off before Rollie could say "bye."

She looked around her room. There were clothes scattered on the floor. Something else Nona would fuss about. She snatched some items and dropped them in the overflowing hamper. Either her grandmother was slacking, or she was waiting on Tai to bring it down. It was a battle Tai could play all day. She packed the clothes tight until the hamper bulged. She checked the room once more, trying to see it through Nona's eyes.

A plastic bag with several hangers caught her eye. Nona had asked her to recycle the dry cleaning stuff last week. She kept forgetting. She grabbed it and raced down the narrow staircase. One of the hangers scraped against the wall like nails on a chalkboard.

"Metai," her grandmother called out. "What I tell you about scratching up my walls?"

"Sorry, Nona," Tai called back upstairs. "I'm going to Bean's."

Before she could race out the door Nona was already coming down the stairs, fingers inspecting the wall. She looked Saturday-morning clean with her hair freshly done, wearing a black T-shirt that hugged her curves and a pair of black linen capri pants. The word *wine-o* and a wine glass were jeweled across her chest. Satisfied there were no scratches, she turned her scowl into a smile.

"You know the supe call himself charging me extra if he has to do anything but repaint," her grandmother said, no longer upset. She spied the hangers jutting out of the recycle bin. "I can't believe it. I didn't have to remind you to recycle that mess. Is my baby girl growing up?"

As bad as Tai wanted to roll her eyes, she let her grandmother win that one. "Um-hm," she said, mostly tuning out Nona's teasing about how that should mean the overflowing hamper should make its way downstairs any day now. She kept her eyes on the action across the street.

Bean was heading inside until Mr. Jamal yelled, "Ay, you forgetting something, Ms. Phillips?" His head gestured to the open hatch of the truck and the dozen or so grocery bags inside.

"I thought that's what dads were for?" Bean teased back.

Metai wasn't positive, but Bean sounded more proper than usual. Looked like being in the Woods all summer had rubbed off on her after all.

Her jet-black micro braids, a big, fragile bun at the top of her head, bobbed as she laughed. She backtracked to cuff three of the bags at a time, then disappeared into the house. Mr. Jamal grabbed up a bunch more, then bellowed for his sons to get the rest.

Tai watched it unfold with restless envy.

They were all corny close. Mr. Jamal never had a problem sending her home when he wanted "Phillips time." Tai always lingered, thinking if she dipped out slow enough Mr. Jamal would include her. Her and Bean were practically sisters, they were together so much. But to her annoyance, he never did. Like, what did they do different when she stepped out of the house, anyway?

She didn't notice her own father, stretched out across Nona's couch, until he propped himself up on one elbow and yelled over to her. "So it's just me and you today, Booty Boo?"

He knew she hated that stupid nickname. She also hated repeating to him how much she hated it. It was like he played dumb on purpose. For real, what grown man enjoyed arguing?

Yet if she said something back, it would be she was acting too grown. Then Nona would start talking yang about respecting her father. And Tai wasn't about to go there. He needed to respect his self first. Grown and still living at home whenever he was in between girlfriends. The latest had kicked him out, probably for being an overgrown child.

His icy mint eyes sparkled as he grinned. They looked so much alike in the eyes, it was like looking in a mirror. The only difference was how his got wider, hers more narrow, when they smiled.

Ignoring him, she frowned at Nona. "Where you going today?"

Nona's arm went around her, escorting her to the sofa so the three of them were huddled. "I'm going to the Food and Wine Fest, baby girl." Nona's arms folded across her chest. "Bryant, didn't I ask you to text Tai earlier this week so you would know what's on her schedule this morning?" She shook her head, disgusted. "Look, I won't be back until about eight or nine. I don't want Tai out there running the streets. I thought you'd made plans, boy."

Tai's mouth disappeared as she pressed her lips together to keep from saying anything. Her father plan something for the two of them? Please. Until she was eight, Tai had thought he was her older brother. He was as useless as one.

Her father didn't even have the good sense to look ashamed. It wouldn't be the first time he hadn't done what Nona had asked him. And her grandmother was a fool on some other level if she thought it was the last.

Tai rushed to get herself out of it. He wasn't the only one who didn't want to be chained together all day.

"I was just going to chill with Bean all day anyway." She barely glanced his way as she pressed. "He can do what he want."

Nona's hands flew to her hips. "Jamila just barely getting home, Metai. I couldn't ask Jamal to watch you all day. The man probably want to spend some time with his daughter."

The truth hit Tai like a hammer to the face. Her father made it worse.

"So you still need me or what, Ma?" He sat up fully alert, smelling a way out. "'Cause I got some business I got take care of down Fourth, anyway."

"The only business you gon' take care of is your child, Bry-ant," Nona said, splicing his name so he knew she wasn't playing.

He looked about as happy about it as Tai. Knowing he wouldn't come up with a convincing enough argument—he never did when he wanted his way—Tai pushed, despite the finality in her grandmother's voice. "Nona, Mr. Jamal already said we could hang out." Her mouth puckered as she forced out the rest. "And if he get tired of me, trust, he'll send me home."

Nona walked into the kitchen. She went about packing a small cooler with waters and fruit. She worked through their small kitchen stacking the cooler far beyond its capacity. Her face was a mix of concentration and frustration.

"Even if you go over for a while, you not staying all day, Tai," Nona said, before whipping around to lash out at her son. "And don't be asking if I need you like you some paid babysitter. Metai is your child. Not mine." She huffed, adding a hasty, "Baby girl, Nona don't mean no harm by that. But your father"—she raised an eyebrow at him—"needs to start taking on more responsibility." She went on muttering, focused on packing. "Boy twenty-eight years old and he gon' sit there and act like he doing me a favor by spending time with the child he done made."

She furiously threw things in the cooler.

Tai's father shook his head, like Nona was the one crazy, and laid back down.

Metai's stomach cramped. She moved away from the sofa and closer to her grandmother's ranting in the kitchen. Whenever her father came around, it always came to this same scene. She wished he'd just stop visiting or whatever he called himself doing. For as much as Nona fussed about wanting him to step up his daddy game, things between them were always better when her father was gone. Tai figured Nona felt guilty. And that was fine. Whatever it was, Nona let her do more and did more for her when time between his drop-ins stretched out.

He always messed stuff up by showing up randomly. She blew out a loud breath to remind her grandmother she was still there.

Nona's face was tight. She put down the cooler, came over, and wrapped her arms around her granddaughter. "Have fun today." She directed her voice to the living room. "You can stay over Bean's till four, then come on home. All right?"

Tai managed to nod over the huge lump in her throat. She didn't return Nona's hug and instead of giving her grandmother a kiss, only put her cheek to Nona's puckered lips. Four o' clock. How was Nona gonna make her sit in the house all day like that?

She shouldered the door open and sulked across the street to Nona's mild reprimand about not getting a kiss back. But when Tai glanced back, the door was already shut.

Her father ruined everything. All he had to do was

act like they had plans. Once Nona was gone, Tai would have been in the wind and he wouldn't have said nothing, because then Nona would have known he didn't have squat planned for them to do. He was so stupid.

Life without him would be perfect, right about now.

CHAPTER
9

The music was sky-high. Mila and Tai were in her room, home alone, removing the last bit of evidence of summer with giant cotton balls and smelly nail polish remover. Mila felt lighter for the first time in hours.

A day really did make a difference.

It was one of those things her dad said to them whenever one of them didn't get their way. Sometimes he acted like he was giving them some kind of prize by letting them be mad or pout as he predicted, "You'll be all right tomorrow. Watch what a difference a day makes."

JJ usually outright disagreed with their dad. Mila

always kept quiet. She couldn't remember the last time any of them had ever changed their dad's mind once it was made up. Besides, he was usually right.

In twenty-four hours she'd gone from feeling hopeless to believing that if she kept to her new plan, everything would work out—she wouldn't go over to Tai's when Mr. Bryant was home. She almost laughed at the simplicity of the plan. Like, duh!

She still wasn't totally sure how she was going to find out if Mr. Bryant was home every single time, or if she'd still go over as long as Ms. Sophia was there. She was leaning toward yes on that second one. But like her dad always said—cross that road when you get to it.

There was also the fact Tai could beat you down with every reason in the book to get you to do things her way. But it had worked with Operation Stop Calling Me That and faster than Mila had expected.

She wasn't blind. It was obvious Tai hated having to remember to call her by her real name. Every time she corrected herself, her mouth would purse like she'd tasted a lemon. But it seemed like she was trying and that was a lot coming from Tai. There was no reason Mission Stick Up for Yourself couldn't work, too.

If anybody knew about all her missions and

operations, they'd think she was crazy. Good thing nobody was peeking into her head.

She sat on her bed, head bopping to the music, swiping the cotton ball over her fingernails. Wearing polish on her nails to dance was like being out of uniform. She might as well show up to ballet in jazz shoes—Mademoiselle would be just as annoyed.

Tai sat across from her on the desk, her feet on the back of the chair, toes wiggling as she painted them.

The entire room was smothered in fumes.

"I can't believe it but I'm ready for school to start," Tai said, talking loud instead of turning down the music that was right beside her.

Mila scrubbed at the stubborn purple stain on her thumb a few more seconds before giving up. Her own feelings about school's pending start were mixed. She liked school. Not loved but liked. It had a familiar and comfortable rhythm that she understood. More importantly, it left only a few hours a day for things to pop off in the hood. Was she ready? Yes. Was she excited? Not about school, really. But she'd awakened with a new thirst for things to be different, and the only change out there was TAG, which, of course, she had zero control over. But again—she'd cross that road when she got to it.

"I guess I am, too," she admitted begrudgingly.

Tai squinted over at her. "You guess? Shoot, usually you have your notebooks, folders, and everything ready." She clasped her hands together and fake begged, "Don't tell me you turning in your teacher's pet card. Don't say it."

Mila threw a cotton ball. Tai batted at it like it could actually reach her from across her room.

Tai could joke all she wanted, but she was closer to the truth than she knew. If Mila could help it, this year was going to be about change. It was their last year in middle school; they weren't kids anymore.

She tested her theory carefully. "I asked my dad if I could move to the Woods for high school—"

"I knew it," Tai declared. Her head shook in disappointment. "I knew you staying over there all summer was just a way to stay in bougie town forever."

Mila snapped back. "Calm down, Tai. He said no." She took a deep breath, hating that she felt like bawling again. She waved her hand in front of her nose, pretending to clear the fumes as she pushed on, trying to sound like none of it mattered. "I'm tired of the Cove. It's the same thing all the time." She glanced up. "Don't you ever wish you could live somewhere else?"

"Hello, have you met my father?" Tai asked, her laugh fake. "When he home, yeah, I wish I lived anywhere else." The nail brush hung over her toe. There was something like sympathy in her eyes, then she blinked and it was gone. "But this our last year at Woodbury, girl. We be in high school soon. That's why I'm excited."

"True," Mila said neutrally.

The nail polish clacked softly as Tai shook the bottle. "The Cove really ain't that bad. Why you so pressed to leave?"

Mila's mind pictured the answer her mouth would never say: "Your father."

She saw Tai's backyard in her mind. The two of them outside, playing. Laughing. Tai's father on the step. Shirtless. He was on the phone, eyes staring past them. Or Mila had thought.

She slammed brakes on the images before they went any further. Even before *it* happened, there wasn't any love for Mr. Bryant in her house. Whenever her dad saw him, he went off like Tai's father's failures were his fault.

Grown man still living at home (sort of).

Irresponsible.

Lazy.

Everything that was wrong with the Cove.

Tai didn't have much love for her father, but how do you tell your best friend her father is the reason you wish you lived somewhere else?

The only other answer Mila could come up with wasn't much better, that getting out of the Cove was normal and staying forever wasn't. Her and Tai saw that differently, for sure. Shoot, Tai still expected her to come over her house as if nothing had happened that day. Hadn't she seen what went down?

Mila was too scared to ask now. Worst, she was afraid if she did, Tai would accuse her of imagining it.

Her arms goose bumped in the warm room. "I figured he'd send me since he sent Cinny." She ended the conversation before hurt could crawl into her voice. "I know it's dumb. Like getting upset when you don't get what you want for Christmas."

It was her turn to fake laugh. She was relieved when Tai ran with it, talking about the year she'd asked for a trip to Disney World and got a gift card to the Disney store. It wasn't funny at the time, but the memory had them rolling. She gladly switched subjects, relieved to talk about something else.

"Isn't it crazy that Chris and Christol came all the way here for TAG? If they really doing cuts, I guess we already know at least two people who gonna make it, huh?"

Tai shrugged, sullen. "I guess. Still stupid to me. It would be a trip if they didn't make it."

"Nah, I can't see that. If anybody getting in, it's them," Mila said, feeling it in her bones. "Maybe they know something we don't, like a secret password or something."

Tai's eyes rolled. "Or maybe it's fixed anyway. To me if they came all this way acting like they have it on lock, it probably is."

"I was only joking," Mila said, confused by Tai's mood change. She was glad when both their phones vibrated, distracting them.

Tai read the Mini Chat message first. She sucked her teeth. "Mo trying get us go to the mall with her."

Mila hopped off the bed and parked herself on the desk next to Tai. She peeked over her shoulder at the Mini Chat. Mo's plans were simple: hit the mall that afternoon to window-shop for school and grab some pizza. It sounded perfect to Mila. She grabbed her own phone and poised her fingers to message back.

"What's wrong with going to the mall? We not doing anything else today," Mila said.

"Mo snap her fingers and we just jump and go?" Tai asked. Her mouth was a stubborn pout. "Besides, Nona said I gotta be back home by four. So—" She typed back: *yall gonna have to roll w/o us. Have fun* ☺

"Really?" Mila asked, reading the message in disgust.

Tai's face was innocent curiosity. "What?"

Mila thrust her phone at Tai. "A smiley face? Like you really care if they have fun."

Tai snickered with a shrug. "Nobody ever mean the emojis they put. What you want me put, the crying one like I care we can't go?"

We. The word felt like a handcuff.

Mila tried sounding normal despite her growing irritation. "What if I wanted to go to the mall?"

"Why you ain't say something then?" Tai asked.

Mila sighed, waiting until there was no breath coming out of her nose before answering calmly. "You didn't give me the chance to. By the time I got my phone, you were texting back."

"Okay. But I can't go to the mall." She folded her arms. "See how Mo be causing drama, though. She never asked, she was just all—ay, let's hit up the mall.

If she had asked, then I could have told her I couldn't go."

Mila was ashamed to feel relief that Tai was taking her anger out on Mo. The two of them were constantly trying to be in charge. Some days Mila felt like her and Sheeda needed an award for putting up with their bossy friends. She took the exit Tai gave her and let the argument rest. It wasn't until much later that she realized Tai had set her up.

What else could she call it when Tai "suddenly" suggested they head over to her empty house to get her phone charger and not even two minutes after they'd walked through the door, Simp and Roland showed up?

Set up. All day.

Mila sat in the living room, mad, one eye on the door. Even though Tai announced that no one was home, Mila couldn't help feeling Mr. Bryant was going to come down the stairs any second, looking half drowsy, as always. She sat on the floor. Her back was against a velvety rocker chair so she could see the entire room—the front door to her left and the stairs to her right. Eventually, being able to see everything calmed her down. She scrolled through her playlist.

Roland and Tai were on the sofa. Simp was kneeled behind it, his elbows on the back like he was at an altar ready to pray. His big head hovered between Roland and Tai. His dreads looked like they were trying to squirm down the couch and onto Tai.

His voice boomed. "Ay, Bean, you playing something today or what?"

"I got it," Mila said. She didn't have the heart to snap at Simp, but that didn't mean she had to answer to him, either.

"Go help her, Simp," Tai said in a sweet voice. "She might even let you if you call her Mila." Mila fussed Tai out with her eyes, but it only encouraged her. "You better check her before she put on some gray music they listening to in the Woods."

The possibility of Mila playing "white" music pushed Simp into action. He walked over, saving the day in his mind, and plopped next to Mila. "Man, don't nobody want hear that white boy stuff."

"I'm good, Simp," Mila said with practiced patience. But he was on a mission to please Tai.

"You got that new Whirl?" he asked.

His arm moved in tiny tics from his wrist until it reached his neck, popping to its own beat. The isolations were precise and clean like there was a slow current of electricity making each part of his arm come alive one second at a time. He was good. Probably good enough to audition for TAG if he could have. He completed his animation by tapping Mila on the shoulder like he was passing the beat on to her. He grinned at her. "Whirl's new jawns is hot."

"Oh my God, jawns is not hot," Tai said. Her scorn was real. "You sound so country. Please don't use that word again."

Simp withered a little but he returned to snooping over Mila's shoulder as if Tai hadn't just reprimanded him like he was a two-year-old. "So you got it?" His breath was warm on her neck.

Mila resisted the urge to wipe off his spittle. She shook her head no, then clicked "Walls Bangin" to get some music on. As it thumped from the speakers, she lowered her voice, so only Simp could hear. "Why do you let Tai talk to you any kind of way, Simp?"

She had her reasons for letting Tai do stuff. But she didn't get why other people did. For a second she thought he might put her question on blast, but he laughed, then imitated her casual low talk. "Shorty don't fade me. Tai all mouth anyway." He pointed to a song on her screen and raised his voice. "Ay, play that. It look like it might be hittin'."

He pushed himself off the floor and went back to his spot behind the couch.

"That drum line is sway," Roland said. "Who dat, Bea . . . Mila?"

Mila smiled. She checked her player. "It's the new one by the Rowdy Boys."

Roland's eyes grew wide. "The new album out?"

Mila shook her head. "No. This is an advance copy. You know, so people can review it or whatever."

Tai scooted closer to Roland. She pressed her leg against his. "Her Aunt Jacqi work for *Mad Shout-out* magazine. She be lacing Jamila with new music all the time."

"Really, Tai? *Jamila?*" Mila gave her a raised eyebrow.

"Now you see how it feels," Tai said playfully. "But I'm kind of liking how that sounds. I think I'm rolling with the government name from now on."

Even if Tai was only joking, the gesture made Mila happy inside like someone had inflated her with helium. She wasn't used to Tai going along with anything she suggested, but she liked how it felt.

She lined up more songs, purposely picking several more Rowdy Boys songs. The music had a grip on Roland. His foot stomped out the song's beat—*boom, tap, boom tap tap*—his head nodded and his arms tapped at an invisible drum. Dance did the same thing to her.

"That's fire right there," he said. He sat up, legs wide, elbows on his knees, and talked over the music. "Auditions in two days. Y'all ready?"

"Here we go," Simp said with a vicious eye roll. "I be glad when these things over, yo."

"It's messed up that you can't try out, B, but don't knock my hustle," Roland said with a sincerity that made Mila envy his honesty. She had never been able to disagree with Tai like that without it turning into an argument.

Simp put his hand out and slid it across Roland's. They gripped at the fingers in a shake. "I ain't hating," Simp said. He sat himself on the back of the sofa and mimed shooting a ball. "The block gon' miss you, though. I'mma ball hard for both of us this season."

Tai looked from Simp to Roland. "Can't you still play basketball even if you do TAG?"

Simp's lip was lifted in a sneer as he quietly shot his imaginary ball. Mila didn't know what it was about, but something changed. Roland looked upset. He gave Simp a look, then shook his head. "I don't know if I can do both. Didn't you read the paper? It's a lot of events, field trips, and stuff you gotta do if you get into TAG."

"Do Martinez know you might not play?" Tai asked, concern in her voice.

"I ain't worried about all that right now," Roland said, clearly agitated.

Tai pressed. "I thought y'all signed contracts and everything."

"People always dipping and diving trying find out stuff that ain't their business," Simp said, scowling, then seemed to realize his sharp tone. "Just saying, there ain't no contract. But if you was recruited, Tez assuming you staying till high school. He definitely gon' be low-key pissed if Rollie quit."

This time Roland didn't hold back. He balled his fist and punched Simp in the thigh hard enough for Simp to yowl "ouch." "Come on, yo, you don't need put my business out there like that."

Simp rubbed at his thigh but remained quiet.

Mila didn't think much of it. Hood basketball was competitive. It was why her dad wouldn't let JJ play for Martinez. He said being that focused on basketball made people forget that there was other stuff more important. She tried to blow away the weird storm cloud.

"Do you have your drum solo ready for the audition?"

At the mention of drumming, Roland's fingers tapped. "Almost. You?"

"I'm just going to do part of the dance we learned for our recital last year," Mila said. Mademoiselle's words about bringing her "A game" replayed. She had practiced once. The reality sent a nervous prick down her back.

Tai broke in. "I'm not even sure I want to do it now. I hate these stupid charity programs. It's just like Girls Up and Brother to Brother. They always trying tell you what to do. How to act." She frowned. "Nona do that just fine."

Simp was quick to agree. "Brother to Brother was wack. I did it for, like, two weeks and was, like . . . get outta here wit' that."

If he had expected Tai to be Team Him, he was disappointed. She elbowed him. "Get off the couch like that. My grandmother would have a fit."

"My bad." He kneeled at the back of the couch and became a giant talking head again. "But for real I'm with Tai. They come up with a new thing every year." His eyes cut Tai's way for approval. When she didn't diss him, he kept on. "If it was for balling that be different." His wrist flicked as he shot his imaginary ball.

"I mean I'm doing it," Tai said, switching sides once more. "I'm just not as pressed as Rollie."

A tiny smile broke across both their faces before Roland corrected her. "Going for what you know ain't the same as being pressed."

"Yeah, yeah," Tai said. She laughed hysterically as Roland tickled her.

Just then, the door crashed open. Mr. Bryant stood just inside the living room, his eyes glazed, taking in the four of them. His body leaned slightly to the left, swaying from an invisible breeze. "Metai, who told you you could have a bunch of hardheads over?" he hollered over the music.

Mila jumped to her feet. She stood, trapped, eyes skating around the room to see what everyone else would do.

Simp popped up. He looked at Roland then Tai, like he was waiting for one of them to do the talking. Roland stood up slow, like he didn't want to make any sudden movements. His hand ran over his shirt, pressing out invisible wrinkles.

Tai was the only one unfazed. "Nona knows Simp and Rollie," she said, not bothering to get up.

Her father's face darkened. He eyed Simp up and

down. "I don't care if she do know 'em. Ain't nobody said nothing about you having company."

Tai's eyes rolled. "So I was supposed to sit in the house by myself all day?"

"You coulda called me and asked was it all right," her father said. His elbow nudged just enough to scoot Simp back a step. "'Scuse me, partner. Do you mind? I'm trying talk to my daughter."

"Mr. Bryant, we was just chilling," Roland said. He extended his right hand. "I'm Roland Matthews from third court."

Mr. Bryant looked at the hand like it was a piece of rotten meat. "Cool, you got manners. Then that means you know how it look when two hardheads up in here with two young girls. I don't care what y'all thought you were doing. But don't be up in my crib chilling when no adults here. Everybody hear that?"

He gave Simp and Roland steely looks until they nodded obediently. He looked over at Mila, as if just realizing she was there.

Her breath caught in her throat.

"Bean, I'm surprised at you. I always expect you to be the one that keep Tai from doing stupid stuff," he scolded.

Her mouth popped open as she considered apologizing, then closed just as fast. She unplugged her player from the speakers. It took her trembling fingers three tries.

Mr. Bryant looked back at Tai. "Wait till I tell Mama. We see how chill you be then."

Tai was up in a flash. Steam was practically coming out of her ears. "How it sound that you my father and you gon' tell on me? You be so pathetic it's not even funny."

Mr. Bryant swayed again like the gale of words had blown into him. This time his right foot stepped out to catch himself before he leaned into the door.

Mila inhaled silently. Her limbs shook at the thought of him running up on Tai and smacking her. After all, he was her father. He could do that.

Would the guys jump in and help?

Would she?

She didn't want to find out. She was torn between trying to protect Tai and getting as far away as soon as possible. Tai saved her from having to make a decision.

"Let me know when you tell Nona so I can be sure to be right there and make it clear to her that if you had been home when I got back from Jamila's, there would have been an 'adult' here." She stormed down the hall.

While he eyeballed her retreat, Mila darted to the door and squeezed by. She squished herself against the doorframe hard, to avoid touching him. A hint of acrid smoke trailed up her nose as she passed him. Mr. Bryant tilted out of the way as Roland and Simp silently followed. Thankfully, he'd lost interest in all three of them.

"Stay your butt up there, too," he yelled up the stairs, slamming the screen door closed behind them.

Nobody said a word until they were safely across the street and on the sidewalk in front of Mila's.

"Man, he a straight a-hole," Simp said.

"He high," Roland said simply. But he looked as shook as the rest of them.

Simp glanced back at Tai's front door. "Maybe we shouldn't leave her in there with him."

"What we gon' do, man?" Roland said, his voice cracking. "That's her father."

Still, he looked back at the door, too.

"Tai knows how he is," Mila said with more confidence than she felt. "He gonna end up laying on the couch and falling asleep." She added bitterly, "I doubt he'll even remember all this when he gets up."

Simp's eyes raised. "I didn't know he still got faded like that, 'cause—"

"Come on, son, let it go," Roland interrupted.

Simp shut right up. They all just stared over at Tai's house.

Regret sat on Mila's shoulder like a gorilla. She should have gone to the mall. Or made up a reason to stay home. Or left Tai's house an hour earlier. She hadn't done anything right. Just went along like always. She just wanted to be home. "I'll talk to y'all later."

Roland's hand grasped her arm. "Hold up a second." He put his hand out and gave Simp a pound, dismissing him. "Ay, I catch up with you in a minute."

"Yeah, all right," Simp said. He stared up at Tai's window as he walked off.

"What's up?" Mila asked, her voice barely above a whisper.

Roland folded his arms across his chest then unfolded them. "You mad at me or something?"

She blinked nonstop as she forced herself to look him in the face. "Why would you think that?"

"'Cause you stopped answering my messages," he said.

She silently let go of the breath she'd been holding. "Oh. I thought maybe somebody had started some nonsense about me." She laughed, the relief real. Cove rumors could start years-long beefs with people.

He did the choppy laugh. "Naw, nothing like that."

Her relief was quickly replaced with dread at Tai knowing about their summer chats. "I know you know that Tai likes you, right?" She met his gaze. It was almost like they were back in the Woods again. He was that easy to talk to when it was just the two of them.

"I might know something about that." A tiny smile spread across his face. Then he got serious. "But what that got do with me and you talking?"

"Everything," Mila said, dead serious. "She's my best friend. I don't want her thinking me and you are scheming behind her back."

His eyes rolled. "I known you just as long as I've known Tai, Bean."

"Yeah, but Tai wouldn't see it that way," Mila said, desperate to make him understand. "Just being honest, but I didn't want it getting back to her that I was talking to you all summer and not texting her, Mo, and Sheeda."

He grinned. "Oh, I was the only one you kept up with while you was gone?"

Mila inhaled sharply. "Roland, for real, don't ever tell Tai that. I mean—" She looked up at Tai's window. "I didn't want you to think I was igging your messages.

But I really wasn't talking to anybody this summer because I was spending time with my sister."

"Yeah, when I saw your FriendMe page wasn't being updated, I was like Oh true, Bean for real for real off the grid."

"We're good, though. I'm not mad," she insisted, twirling a braid around her finger.

"Good." He started to settle into a conversation when the door to Tai's house slammed shut. They both watched as Mr. Bryant came onto the front stoop. He lit a cigarette, blowing the smoke in their direction. He stared squarely at Roland, but to Mila his eyes were hooks digging into her. She backed slowly toward her door.

"All right, Roland, I'll see you later," she said.

Roland stood on the sidewalk for a few more seconds, staring confused at Tai's father. Even through the door Mila could feel Mr. Bryant's gaze. She turned on every light in the house and waited in her room, as far away from the front of the house as possible, for her dad and the boys to return.

It turned out, sometimes even a few days or months didn't make a difference.

CHAPTER 10

Regrets was for suckers.

Tai didn't regret the ugly fight she'd had with her father in front of everybody. He was a butt, plain and simple.

The second Nona walked in, Tai had raced to the door bawling that he'd embarrassed her in front of her friends. She played it up with dripping snot from her nose, twitchy eyes, and pretending to be afraid to look at her father.

Nona had gotten hot when she realized he hadn't been home already. She'd lectured him so hard he finally stormed out. He never got the chance to snitch about Simp and Rollie being there.

That's what you get, Tai thought with stubborn satisfaction.

It was two days later and she was basically the winner, but the whole scene still hurt. Of all people for him to act like a tail in front of, it had to be Rollie.

But nope, she didn't regret it because Rollie had checked in on her the rest of the night, low-key asking was everything cool. Him caring if she was cool made the whole stupid thing worth it. Now they were on Skyvo making moves for the day.

They weren't even talking about anything, for real. She didn't care as long as he didn't log off, but she moved her face up to the camera and put on a pretend pouty voice. "Hello? Why you ain't saying nothing?" then went right back to texting Bean so she wouldn't just be staring at the screen while he played whatever video game he was into. His fingers clicked and clacked on the controller, working it hard while she tried to get Bean to hit center court.

JahMeeLah: *I don't feel like it.*

Tai's fingers slid across the screen, swiping her message into existence: *OMG so whut u gon sit in the house every day til school?!!! Cmon. Rollie coming if I can get him off Skyvo. Lolz*

JahMeeLah: *It's hot Tai!!* 🔥

DatGirlTai: *So!!! Cmon*

Tai paused for a second then texted: *Please*

She hated begging. Why did Bean always have to make hanging out so hard?

"Like, just come on, girl," Tai muttered to herself.

Any other time she would have said that to Bean, but things were different lately. A few times she'd caught Bean frowning like Tai was getting on her nerves even when Tai couldn't think of anything she'd said wrong.

All these years she'd been the mouthpiece and Bean her quiet backup. Now she didn't know what her friend was thinking anymore. Both of them couldn't be the lead, snapping on people and setting them straight. Not that Bean was even capable of that.

She mock-complained to Rollie, hoping for sympathy. "Bean be so irky sometimes. She never want be out in the cut."

Rollie eyed the screen over his shoulder. It was only the second time he'd looked away from his game. Tai lifted up her chin, lowered her eyes, and gave him a pout for good measure. She hoped her lips looked kissable.

"For her being your girl, you mad hard on her." He snorted. "That wouldn't be me."

"Like you don't be dogging Simp. And that's supposed to be your boy." She palmed the camera, giving it a smush. "Whatever, boy. Bye."

"Please, I don't do Simp like that," Rollie said. "If he not down to hang, that's on him. I don't trip over it."

He reared back in his chair, arms tight, fingers tapping furiously. When he accomplished whatever had set him off, he talked easily like he'd never stopped. "Just saying, everybody know you and Mila tight. But you always coming for her. Seem messed up to me."

Tai wasn't trying to get into it with him even though she hated being talked to like that with a passion. If it had been anybody else, she would have gone off. She couldn't help that Bean was the quiet one, as everybody loved to say. Like being quiet won you money or something. Hello, quiet didn't get Rollie hitting you up on Skyvo, did it?

Everybody had a job to do in a friendship, just like it was Simp's to jibber jabber away so Rollie could play that quiet, intelligent thing he was always doing. There was something about Rollie. She didn't think he was as quiet as he came off. There was a wild boy in there somewhere and she was determined to get closer and find out for herself. The thought made her tingle inside. She put the whole matter to rest. She didn't want to argue with Rollie.

"Look, ain't nobody coming for Bean," she said, meaning it. "But we only have three weeks left of summer. I'm ready get out and chill." She pulled herself from the screen and went about picking an outfit. "She did what she wanted this summer. Can't I have these last few days? I mean, dang." Her exasperation was real.

Hearing Rollie laugh broke up her bitterness. His laugh was so cute, all low and raspy.

She walked away from the screen so Rollie wouldn't see her grinning. It would blow her whole playing-it-cool vibe.

He teased her, talking about how she knew she was wrong. Ignoring him, she picked through potential camisoles to wear. But her eyes narrowed in concentration when Rollie's voice, floating through the tiny speaker holes right in her direction, said, "Shoot, from what I know, she loved it over there. When I saw her that night, for real she looked like a different person . . . acted like it, too."

Tai's hand dropped to her waist, like the cami weighed a hundred pounds.

When he saw who? They'd been talking about Bean. Had he jumped conversations on her? She stayed mute and off to the side so he couldn't see her confusion. She grabbed a pair of jean shorts to ride with the cami.

"I ain't never really seen Bean smile that much." He paused, then added quickly, "No shade, though. It was good to see her laugh. She be so serious, always."

Tai slipped out of her pajamas, tempted to flash Rollie a taste, then decided against it. Just her luck, Nona would roll in. Staying well away from the bubble of the camera lens, she dropped the cami over her head and was still buttoning her shorts, her game face back on, when she plopped down in front of the screen.

"Oh, you saw her this summer? When?" she asked, using all her will to keep her right eyebrow from arching, a telltale sign she was mad.

Rollie's eyes widened. "Snap, you was getting dressed?"

Her need for information too deep to flirt back, Tai only nodded.

"Oh, so you were naked while I'm sitting right here?" A smirk lifted the corner of his mouth, followed by a grin that warmed Tai, even almost threw her off course. But the anger bubbling in her chest wouldn't let it.

"Um-hm," she said, at least remembering to smile back. "So when you see Bean, though?"

He frowned. His finger tapped firmly, once, and the

noise from the game silenced. Finally he shrugged as he gave up searching for the answer.

"I forget when, for real. It was twice, though." His head went off screen as he bent down. When he appeared again he was standing. Tai had to lean in to hear because his mic wasn't getting his voice as good. "The first time I was over my cousin Michael's house. He live with his grandmother over there in the Woods." He walked away from the screen. His voice came back even more distant, but Tai heard him. She was nearly glued to the screen. "Then I ran into her at the Garret Carnival. . . . "

Everything after that was sounds and fuzziness.

With questions and voices banging in her head she got through another few seconds, making him promise to head to the court, before logging off in a flurry. She texted Bean and promised that they would only stay at the court for a little bit and to just "COME ON." The demand did the trick. Bean agreed to hang.

Questions rolled in Tai's head like scattering bowling pins. Before she could answer one, another landed. One came over and over . . .

Bean had kept this from her. Why?

CHAPTER
11

Mila knew something was up the second Tai stepped out of the house. Her round face was serious and unsmiling. She didn't look like somebody who had just been talking to a dude she'd been crushing on forever. They walked in silence.

The sun was so blazing even the birds were too hot to chirp. Like it always was midday, the hood was quiet. Mila wondered why she agreed to come out. August was confusing. Mornings were cool enough to fool you into wanting a jacket. But by noon the late summer sun was back. Over in the Woods the shade from thick trees made the heat bearable. If she'd still been there, she would have spent the day out back reading with only the crickets for company. There was nowhere to hide from the sun in the Cove. She wiped at the sweat trickling down her neck. Summer heat and Tai had a 'tude. Great.

They passed four houses, five, then six before Mila asked, "You all right?"

No answer. It was so quiet, Mila could hear their footsteps. She counted to fifteen in her head and was up to twenty-five before Tai's high-pitched laugh broke the silence.

"Yeah, girl, I'm good." Her eyes disappeared into slits as she smiled big. "I was ready lay you out for not wanting to hit the court, but whatever. Same ol' Bean never want roll through the hood." She put her hand up. "My bad, same old Jamila."

Mila was so relieved that she ignored the sarcastic way Tai said her name, drawing out the "meel" like if she said it the right way she might turn into dust and blow away.

They walked in sync as Tai gave every detail of her Skyvo with Roland. Before long Mila tuned out, dropping in only to agree that it definitely seemed like he was feeling Tai.

When they arrived at center court, Mo and Sheeda were two lonely specks on the long rows of silver bleachers. Sheeda sat between Mo's legs, her head bent and face hidden by her thick Senegalese twists. Mo's hands pulled and twisted the hair into a complicated updo. Every now and then she looked away to watch the boys hustle up and down the hot court.

As Mila's and Tai's feet banged hollow on the bleachers, Sheeda peeped up from beneath the curtain of hair. "What's up, girlies?"

Mo pushed at her neck. "Keep your head down."

Tai frowned down at Sheeda's mop of hair. "I know those gotta be hella hot." She flicked at the space where her hair used to be. "I'm loving my short hair."

Mo's face contorted as a disobedient twist slid out of her hands. "That's why I'm trying help her put it up. She was making me hot just looking at it."

Mila felt Sheeda's pain. Mo and Tai never wore braids or fake hair. Sheeda and Mila never wore anything but. Mila wanted to wear her hair flat-ironed or curled but once Cinny had moved, it was easier for her dad to send her to get the hair redone every six weeks. She was old enough to take care of it herself, but he kept making the appointments and she was reluctant to tell him she was tired of the style and of sitting in the braiding salon for eight hours every seventh Saturday.

She envied Mo's messy bun. Easy, cool, and cute. She sometimes imitated the style with her own horde of braids. But the hair was too heavy. Instead, her micro braids were wrapped several times and twined with three headbands to keep any of the hot fake hair from making her neck sweat worse. She came to Sheeda's defense.

"All of us don't have the slick and wavy like Tai or the creamy cracked-out perm like you, Mo."

Mo whooped laughter. "Not the creamy cracked-out perm, though."

They joked back and forth as Mila and Tai watched Sheeda's hair transform into a series of thick brown ropes. She looked like she was wearing a hat. Once Mo was done, they watched the boys more closely. Even in the heat they were balling hard like someone was scouting them.

Mila was wondering aloud how long they planned to stay when Christol walked to the court's edge. She wore a pair of obviously homemade jean shorts. The shorts made her long body look even longer. The dangling frayed edges covered more thigh than the denim. Her hair, brushed just past her shoulders, was flat-ironed and bumped at the ends. It looked freshly done and shone in the bright sun like it had been sprayed with oil.

She stood at the end of the bleachers watching her brother and the other boys run up and down the court, clapping and hollering for the ball. Every now and then she glanced back at the girls. Before Mila could wave her over, Christol's eyes swept quickly back onto the court's action.

She gave her credit for coming to the court alone. Unless she was deaf, dumb, and blind, she probably felt the thick pettiness in the air around them. Mostly from Tai, but it wasn't like anybody else had rolled out the red carpet.

Tai's head nodded Christol's way. "So what y'all think about her?" She was smug like she already knew the answer.

Mo folded her arms. "I think I need to work hard to make sure she don't get my spot in TAG. Nothing personal, though."

"Nobody care about no TAG." Tai scowled. "I mean, what you think about her, period?"

"I don't know." Mo put her hand above her eye, shielding the sun. She peered over at Christol. "I haven't seen her except in dance class. She stay inside, I guess."

"I would, too. We're acting all shady like she's done something to us," Mila grumbled.

Tai got extra loud. "This our hood. If she want be down, then she need to do whatever to be down."

Sheeda laughed. "And what's that?"

Tai's eyebrows arched. It seemed like she actually thought about it for a minute before snorting a laugh and coming up with, "Whatever we say."

Tai said some off-the-wall stuff sometimes. Mila and Sheeda didn't always agree with the things Tai said, but they rarely debated her. Mo didn't mind debating but mostly just gave Tai a look that Mila always took to mean *You're wrong but I don't feel like fussing right now.* Because when Mo wanted to fuss, she did.

Mila took Mo's straight-face silence as a good sign. "It doesn't have to be like that, y'all."

Tai sat up taller. "Be like what?"

The familiar challenge in Tai's voice was supposed to be her signal to back down. They were supposed to always be on the same page in public. But how could things change if she just went along every time they didn't agree? She risked Tai's wrath.

"Be petty just because we can. Like Karissa and Jalessa did us our first year at Woodbury, acting like we had to go through them just to breathe." She avoided Tai's disapproving glare by looking to Sheeda and Mo for help. Remembering how much sixth grade sucked pushed her on. "I hated it. We all did. We don't need to act like that with Christol."

"I'm not acting any kind of way," Sheeda said weakly.

Mo pursed her lips. "I already told you I don't know the girl. . . ." She hunched down so she was talking into their circle and lowered her voice. "But it's on her if she want be friends. She the one standing over there by herself."

Sensing Mo was on her side, Tai agreed. "Bean, you can be Frannie Friend to whoever you want. But I don't have to be her friend just because we live in the same hood." She crossed her legs with a prim uppityness.

Quiet fury burned Mila's throat as she asked, "For real, would any of y'all just walk up to four girls you didn't know and push into their convo?"

"I mean, probably not," Mo muttered.

Sheeda stayed quiet, eyes ping-ponging between everyone like she wasn't sure which side to choose.

"If I ain't want be looking dumb by myself forever, yeah," Tai said.

Mila tore her eyes away from Tai's tapping leg and waved Christol over before she thought over it too much. "Christol . . . hey, come sit with us."

"Bean," Tai snapped under her breath. "Why you do that?"

"Let's at least get to know her before we throw shade," Mila said. She breathed in and out through her nose, trying to steady her racing heart. She was sure Tai was burning a hole in the back of her head with her look. She faked a smile and kept her face turned toward Christol, who slowly made her way to the foot of the bleachers. Mila scooted over, inviting her to sit beside her, needing the comfort of the contact.

"Hey y'all," Christol said with a wave.

Everybody except Tai said "hey" back.

"So you named after that Champagne rappers used to talk about?" Sheeda asked with a genuine curiosity that made Mila want to hug and shush her at the same time.

"Probably. It's not spelled the same, though," Christol said with patience and a tiny crescent moon smile. "You can call me Chrissy."

"It's kind of crazy how long you've been dancing," Mo said in open admiration, and Mila knew everything would be okay. She let herself breathe.

"I've never done nothing else," Christol said, proud without bragging.

"Shoot, your mother must be rich then," Sheeda said. She leaned her elbows back on the burning bench, winced, then sat back up. "If it wasn't for Ms. Noelle, no way I could be in dance."

"I know that's right," Mo said.

Mila smiled gratefully at her friends. If they had clammed up and expected her to start the conversation she would have died on the spot. Before she could jump in, Tai did what Tai did best—start drama. Her ticking leg wagged even harder.

"Puh. Please. If her mother was rich, she wouldn't be living here."

"That couldn't be more obvious," Christol said.

"What does that mean?" Tai's voice carried across the empty bleachers. "You trying say we all poor here?"

"Oh my God, Metai, simmer down." Mo laughed. "You the one who said the girl's mother can't be rich. Now she agreeing and you all *rrrr, rrrr, rrrr.*"

Her and Sheeda whooped loud and open at the joke.

Mila envied that they had each other in Tai's storms. She stayed quiet, not smiling or agreeing in any way even as she silently applauded Mo.

"My mother work two jobs so I can dance and so Chris can do music and play ball," Christol said. "Getting into TAG could save money on dance classes. That's why I'm pressed to make it." She turned to Mila. "So how long you been dancing? Your double pirouettes are so good."

"Two years," Mila said, managing not to cheese her butt off at the compliment.

Christol's mouth dropped. "For real?"

Mo teased. "Mila's what they call a 'natural.'"

Mila waved away the praise, embarrassed by it as much as it swelled her with pride.

"For two years you're really good," Christol said. "You trying out tomorrow, right?"

"Why is every conversation about TAG this and TAG that?" Tai exploded.

Everyone stared at her wide-eyed as she ranted.

"Y'all acting like TAG gonna get you jobs dancing in a video or something." She smirked. "I don't mean no harm, Bean, but it's just another one of the ideas that your father always be coming up with trying save the neighborhood." She raised her arms. "Save it from what? We fine here, except maybe you. You the only one unhappy here. So go."

"Girl, what are you talking about? Why you say that?" Sheeda asked. She looked torn between laughing and being worried.

Mila snipped back, "And you know I would if I could."

"I wish you could, too," Tai said with extra bite. "Then everybody could stop always having to worry about saying or doing the wrong thing around you."

The words made Mila's ears ring. When had Tai ever worried about saying the wrong thing to anybody? When did she ever worry about anybody else, period?

"Me?" She clasped her hands on her chest in dramatic sarcasm. "I'm the one people gotta tiptoe around? Wow."

Beside her, Christol leaned her elbows on her knees and stared straight ahead at the basketball court. Mila felt bad for inviting her over. She and Tai had never fought in front of everyone before. She wanted to stop it. Christol probably thought they were all crazy. But the snowball rolled down the hill getting bigger.

Tai's eyes were glazed over. Mila knew the look. She was trying to act like she didn't care. Just in case Mila didn't notice she didn't care, she scooted down, putting distance between them on the seat. "I know you not trying say I'm like that." Tai's voice was tight.

Every word coiled to bite. "As long as people say stuff to my face, they can say whatever they want."

"Yeah, you took me asking you to stop calling me Bean real good. And *that* was to your face," Mila said. The words were out before she had completed the thought. Her throat closed. It was all going so wrong so fast.

She took comfort knowing that if things got too ugly, Mo would step in. For now, she only watched them with furrowed brows, mouth slightly open.

Sheeda, on the other hand, looked like she had shrunk an inch. She was leaning back, burning bleachers or not, as if she was afraid sitting up near the circle of conversation would force her into it.

Mila threw her hands up in surrender, intending to squash the disagreement. "All right, Tai. Naw, you're right." But Tai couldn't even win graciously.

"Exactly. 'Cause I'm the realest chick out here." She pierced Mo and Sheeda with a look, then threw daggers at Christol like it was her fault they were arguing.

Christol sat on the edge of the bleacher. Her eyes followed her brother from one end of the court to the other. Mila expected her to call out to him and run from the madness.

"Nobody saying you fake, Tai," Sheeda said, trying to help.

But Tai wouldn't be calmed. She jabbed her finger at Mila. "She is. She trying say people gotta watch what they say around me. Since when?"

Mo playfully pushed Tai's leg. "Stop. Don't even come for her like that. Bean always been the chill one." She flashed a confident smile Mila's way. "Ain't nobody mad. Let her live."

"Oh please." Tai sneered. "Jah-meel-ah from these streets just like the rest of us. Youn think she can get grimy?"

"So now we name-calling?" Mila asked. The words croaked out of her dry throat. "How am I grimy, Tai?"

Tai did the prissy leg cross again. Her foot swayed softly like she didn't have a care in the world. "'Cause I think the real reason you like the Woods so much is 'cause you can do your dirt over there and nobody be knowing."

Mo stood up, her hands out like a school crossing guard.

"Okay . . . what in the world y'all talking about?" She looked from Mila to Tai, unsure who to start with before deciding on Tai. "Tai, stop being salty and just say what's what. We don't need start the school year on no drama stuff."

"Um-hm . . . Jamila got grimy in her." Tai's mouth was pooched like she smelled bad fish. "Ask her who she kicked it with this summer and ain't tell nobody?"

The sound of the boys' sneakers shuffling on the court and the tingy pounce of the ball filled the silence. All eyes were on her, except Christol. Mila absently moved closer so their legs touched and sent up a silent prayer of thanks when Christol didn't scoot away.

"Rollie, that's who," Tai blurted triumphantly. She joined the circle completely until her knees touched against Mila's. "Now we supposed to be girls and you ain't tell me that you ran into the dude I'm crushing on . . . not once but twice. Tell me that ain't grimy, Jamila."

Mila's head swam. God, had she forgotten to tell Roland not to mention them running into each other? Keeping up with lies was hard.

"It wasn't even like that," she whispered.

"Then what was it like?" Tai asked.

"Whoa, whoa, wait," Mo said. She peered at Mila. "So, like, did you and Rollie hook up?"

Mo's eyes softened when Mila shook her head no.

Tai wasn't having it. Her arms flailed as she folded and unfolded them. "Mo, don't even sit up here and act like that don't make it wrong. How long have I liked Rollie?"

"For forever," Sheeda said with an eye roll.

"Exactly," Tai said, missing Sheeda's sarcasm. "So I don't care what happened or didn't happen. You was wrong for hiding it from me."

"I didn't hide it," Mila said, blanching at the lie. "I just never got the chance to tell you."

Sheeda readily agreed. "I mean, she was away all summer."

Tai shut her down with an icy look. "Please. She never got the chance because she never texted me back. Always too busy doing this with Aunt Jacqs and too busy doing that with Cinny."

The words dug into Mila like a knife, twisting. She shot up off the bleacher, towering over Tai. The motion surprised Mo into sitting back down. Mila's voice matched Tai's accusing tone. "So my real crime is I went to my aunt's instead of being your shadow all summer." The shock on Tai's face spurred her on. "I can't help that you don't have any brothers or sisters or that your father always high."

Mo inhaled sharply.

"Oh God," Sheeda groaned.

The words that had been welled up inside of Mila wouldn't stay down. Tai said whatever she wanted, no matter how mean, like it was okay just because it was how she felt. It wasn't. It never had been, but Mila had never said anything, until now.

"Nobody can say what they want around you because you always got something to say about everything." She paused. "If you don't want to do it or don't like it, it's wack or dumb. You don't even care if you're putting down something somebody else likes. It's played out."

"Ohhh. So somebody finally got enough nerve to say how she feel to my face," Tai said. Her voice was shaky through her set jaw. "That's messed up about you, Bean."

Mila lost it. "Stop calling me 'Bean.'" Her voice was so loud the boys looked up from the court. She dug her fists into her thighs. "How am I the one that's messed up because I'm being honest?" she asked. Controlling the anger made her cheeks hurt.

"Oh, now you being honest?" Tai's laugh was big and phony. "That's right. . . ." She paused, then spit out Mila's name. "Jamila, go ahead and play the shy 'who, me?' role. That's what you do best."

With that, she stormed down the bleachers.

"Tai, don't be like that," Mo called after her. She turned to Mila, sighing. "Go make her come back."

Tai stood at the edge of the gate, where Christol had stood just minutes ago. Every few seconds she swiped at her face. She was crying. It made Mila want to obey Mo's request. Then it struck her. Tai was wrong. What Mila really did best was play nice, every time. All the time. She'd played nice, grateful when Tai said she'd try and remember to stop calling her Bean. And she'd played nice for months pretending that it didn't make her sick to her stomach to sit in Tai's room, wondering if Mr. Bryant would wander up there trapping her exit.

She couldn't play nice today. She shook her head. "Mo, I didn't do anything wrong."

Mo's eyes flickered surprise. She silently walked down to Tai, where they talked in low voices. Every now and then Mo would look up, her eyes pleading with Mila to join her.

Mila stayed put. If she gave in now, she'd never stand up for herself again. Then the Cove would eat her alive. She knew it like she knew the sun would rise each day.

Not this time.

CHAPTER
12

Tai had been to the Players Cultural Arts Center twice. Once in third grade, for a field trip to see a play where everybody on stage wore big horse heads that looked heavy, then another time to watch her cousin graduate from high school. Both times had been boring, boring, boring. The only exciting thing that had ever happened there was when her favorite go-go band, the Rowdy Boys, had a concert. Not that she knew for sure it had been exciting because Nona hadn't let her go. She'd been all, "Too much fighting break out at those go-go's," not even giving Tai a chance to explain that it wasn't one of those fake concerts at a tiny Elks lodge crowded with more people than the fire department allowed. The TRB show was a real concert with an opening act and everything. Plus the Rowdy Boys were a *boy* go-go band. How much fighting did Nona think was going to break out among a bunch of twelve-year-olds? But Tai hadn't been able to convince her.

She was still a little salty about it. Low-key she had a crush on the lead dude and nobody would ever convince her that Nona hadn't ruined her chance to run into him so he could autograph her Rowdy Boys T-shirt. Seeing the building come into view reminded her of the missed concert, souring her already bad mood.

Everybody else around her was losing their minds. It was so loud the bus driver had yelled at them the entire trip. He started out polite-ish with "quiet down," but the last demand was a straight "y'all kids need to shut up." Nobody listened. The entire bus was jacked up.

Two long lines of buses crawled into the circular lot in front of the arts center, pulled up to a set of double doors, unloaded, then moved on. To Tai it seemed like there were thousands of kids streaming into the building.

Why was she doing this again?

Then Rollie's hands tapped out a beat on his lap, reminding her exactly why she was stuck on a bus, at the end of summer break, in the morning like it was a school day. She'd gotten herself into this by lying about being hyped to audition.

It wouldn't have been so bad if her and Jamila weren't fighting.

It was official, she couldn't call her Mila. It was Jamila or nothing. And in her head she was Bean and always would be. Not that it mattered right now. They weren't talking. Now her mind was cramped. Every time she tried to get into the mood for auditions, the argument flashed, shutting down every other thought.

She turned her head as far left as she could, pretending to check out the chaos outside. From the side of her eyes she could see Bean, four rows back, her braided bun bent in conversation with Christol.

She still couldn't believe she hadn't gotten a text from her the night before or even word one while they were at the bus stop. It blew Tai. They had stood right next to each other at the bus stop, so it wasn't like there wasn't a chance to say boo, hello, dog—anything. Instead, everyone else had talked around them trying to crystal ball how the day was going to go. Now she was friended up with new girl. It was like she had been waiting on a reason to cut Tai off.

Disgust and sadness mixed sourly in her stomach as she willed herself not to care. The bus doors opened. She followed behind Rollie and instinctively reached for his hand so he could pull her through the crowd. He grabbed it lightly, pleasing her.

Noelle was obviously in charge. She barked out orders to the herd of students shuffling through the doors. "We need everyone in the auditorium, please." She pointed as she spoke, directing the mass of kids toward a handful of faculty also signaling which way to go. Her eyes lit on Tai, then immediately went over her head and brightened. "Mila. Well, good morning. I'm so glad to see you."

Tai's face burned at being ignored.

"You all right?" Rollie asked. His fingers wiggled in protest inside her death grip.

"Sorry." Tai eased up. She cocked her head in Noelle's direction, straining to catch the rest of the conversation. She filtered out enough sound around her to catch Bean saying, "If you love it, work for it, right?" then there was laughter.

"Good luck" was the last thing Tai heard Noelle say before Rollie led her into the packed auditorium.

A horrifying creep burned in Tai's throat. She folded herself into the auditorium's worn velvet-covered seats and eyed the huge crowd, trying not to think about how much she wanted to cry.

Rollie's head rolled on his neck as he took in everything. "Yo, this is insane. I ain't think it would be this many people trying out. It's a good two hundred people in here."

It seemed like way more. Students stretched from the back row to the front in the cavernous room. She counted them in her head. She stopped at seventy bun heads, afraid to know how many people she was up against.

Until they arrived, one thought had coursed through her mind—there would be enough slots for everybody. Almost all the other bogus keep-the-kids-off-the-street programs accepted everybody. Why would TAG be any different? A few times she'd even thought about bringing that up whenever they talked about TAG. But seeing the clique sweat it out had been kind of fun. They were all so pressed.

Until she'd seen the rows of buses and the

auditioners streaming into the arts center like an army of ants, she'd been convinced she'd have the last laugh. But seventy girls?

At least seventy, she corrected herself. There were more. A lot more based on the number of dancer types she'd watched come off buses in their black leotards, pink tights, and SPANX shorts.

This was real. Everybody wasn't gonna make it.

She inhaled, held her breath, and counted until the burning made its way to the pit of her stomach. A parade of folks came across the stage, singing the praises of TAG. They all sounded too excited and way too rehearsed, like the program was magic.

As stupid as it seemed, Tai wished that it were. If TAG was magic, it could fix her friendship and make things the way they used to be. She tried to put the thought out of her mind, but a surge of hope lifted her spirits. If her and Jamila both made it, they would still be together after school. Eventually things would get better. They had to.

Another thing hit her. Sitting there in the dim auditorium meant Bean had been dead wrong about Tai never going along with anything anybody else wanted to do. As much as she hated ballet, she was here trying out with everybody else, wasn't she? That had to count for something.

When Bean stopped tripping, Tai planned on reminding her of that.

Stubborn satisfaction eased her nerves. Beside her, Rollie's eyes glittered. He was hanging on every word. She breathed quietly through her nose and listened to the millionth person get up and talk about how happy they were to bring this program to them. Good luck. Break a leg. Yadda yadda.

They were finally dismissed into several long lines, including one where they took pictures of everyone auditioning. Eventually she found herself in a dance room trying to decide where to post herself. The room was wall-to-wall dancers and more trickled in behind her.

People were stretched out, legs open in splits, some with one leg on a wall, the other on a partner helping them to loosen up. She stepped over arms and legs, looking for an empty space.

Her shoulders actually jumped when Mo called her name and waved her over to a corner.

Bean and Christol were with her. For a second she debated waving Mo over to sit where she stood, ankle deep in other dancers. But she wasn't beefing with Mo and besides, Mo had called her, so she walked, back straight, face blank. She didn't need Bean thinking she cared about having to sit near her.

She slumped down under the barre, where the girls were camped out. "Like, could there be any more people in here?" she asked, forcing herself to sound normal.

A few girls looked over with mild interest, then went back to stretching.

Tai's head turned every which way, looking back over the sea of dancers.

"Where's Sheeda?" she asked, talking only to Mo.

Mo's chest was lowered down to the floor. She reached for her heels as she answered. "She decided to only try out for drama." She lifted her head long enough to frown at Tai. "For real, I think she thought y'all was gonna do that together."

Tai glanced over at Chrissy Whatsherface almost hoping she'd be looking her way so she could grit on her. But she was facedown in a center split. Why did Mo have to say all that in front of her?

"I can try out for what I want, Monique." She waved her hand at the girls in the room, dismissing them all.

"I'm probably as good as some of these girls."

The look of doubt on Mo's face made Tai hot with anger. She scowled back. "Maybe not ballet, Mo. But I tear jazz and hip-hop up and you know it."

Mo nodded and put her head back down to the floor.

Tai envied her flexibility. She steepled her feet together and bent over them until her nose hovered over the floor. It was the only stretch that made her feel like she was doing something, even though Noelle made it clear it was only stretching out her back.

A voice came from above her. "Do you want some help stretching out?"

A grin leaped across Tai's face.

That's right, Jah-Mee-Lah, you spoke to me first, she thought with cold glee. Her stomach flipped with joy. She fought the urge to snap off a smart answer by only shaking her head no. When Bean's feet didn't move, Tai lifted her head long enough to mumble, "I got it," before bending back down.

She felt hopeful. Bean was the peacemaker. It's just how she was. An apology had to come next. And Tai was ready. Once Bean apologized, she'd go along. Cross her heart and hope to die, she'd squash the beef right then and there. Her eyes stayed on the clean, pink leather ballet slippers as she waited on her friend to dead the tension between them. She counted slowly and was up to fifteen when they padded softly away, disappearing from sight. Tai swallowed against the lump of disappointment searing her throat.

"I tried," she heard Bean whisper softly.

The quiet statement roared in Tai's ears. She tried? Tried what? Tai wondered. Offering some funky little help with stretching wasn't the same as saying you was sorry. And why was she saying that to Christol? Had the two of them been talking about the stupid argument behind her back?

She clamped her jaw so tight it hurt, staying in her sloppy stretch until her back ached. She didn't feel like talking to anyone anymore. Thankfully three teachers strutted in, heads erect. Tai popped up, more than ready to get it all over with.

The teachers stood in the front, stone-faced, until there was absolute silence. None of them were Noelle. Tai wasn't sure if she was relieved or disappointed. At least she knew Noelle's warm-up . . . sort of.

She eyed them carefully. Dance buns always made dancers look older, but she was sure that at least two of the "teachers" were only about sixteen years old. That made her feel better. They probably weren't there to judge her.

She kept her eye on the girl closest to her side of the room. She had on a fierce grape-colored leo—lace in the front with spaghetti straps. The kind of leotard Tai had begged Nona to let her have, but Nona said it was too grown.

The teacher's voice vibrated off the dance room's ceilings. Even in the back, Tai heard her clearly. "We'll do a routine warm-up. One I'm sure will be no issue for those with experience." She wrapped her arms around her small body, nodding gently with every word like she was going down some checklist in her head. "For those who are brand-new to dance, do your best to keep up. Right now, trying is just as important as previous knowledge. The panelists will ultimately be looking at a variety of things, including experience, potential, and heart."

A tiny smile broke across Tai's face. Heart was being courageous enough to try. And it was the one thing Noelle praised her for anytime they had to put all the combinations together and dance across the floor. At first Tai thought she was trying to joke her. But after it happened a few times, she began owning how Noelle would yell over the music, "Girls, be more courageous, like Metai. Do the steps like you know them, even if you don't."

Christol might have the experience. Mo had the potential. And Bean was naturally good, but Tai knew nobody had more heart than she did. And if heart counted, she had this.

Music exploded overhead.

Tai stared a hole into Purple Girl, who demonstrated each step at the very second the older woman called out a move. They were so in sync, Tai had to remind herself to participate and not just stare. She turned off her mind until all she saw was Purple Girl. She imitated her every move until her body felt like it was attached to the girl's body.

She had to get this right. She had a feeling her and Bean's friendship depended on it.

CHAPTER
13

With every move, Mila's heart swooned. She wasn't inside of her body anymore. Instead, she watched every pas de chat, every jeté from above. She didn't know if her arms or legs were right. All she knew was, it felt good. Free.

There were a lot of positions, but the choreography was actually pretty easy. Because of the new girls, she figured.

A smile burst across her heart as she remembered she was still "new" to dance herself.

Ms. Rexler, the audition director, yelled combinations

and counts, keeping the girls as in sync as possible. She demanded the girls extend, move faster, move slower— dance, execute, remember this is an audition. And with every command, Mila adjusted, letting her body be clay formed by the older woman's words.

After the warm-ups, with everyone still panting to catch their breath, four panelists including Mademoiselle Noelle walked into the room and took their places at a long table in the front of the room. They had clipboards and cups and marched in as if someone had given them a cue. No one said anything.

Mila wanted to look at Mademoiselle but was afraid. It would only make her more nervous. She watched, hawklike, as the first line of girls went, then the second. She named every step they did, banging it into her memory.

Her line was third. It gave her legs a chance to steady. Not much, but enough.

The music started.

The song eased into Mila's ear and seeped into her bloodstream. She moved naturally to the beat until the song cut off abruptly. When it did, she stood, heels touching in first position, waiting for instruction. The girls on either side of her breathed hard. She slowed her breath until she was breathing in time with them. She was afraid to breathe too loud in case Ms. Rexler or the judges said something.

Mademoiselle Noelle leaned over and pointed to something on her paper. She flicked her eye up at a girl to Mila's left. The judge nodded. "Again, please," Mademoiselle said, tenting her hands in front of her.

The music started then seemed to stop even faster than before. Mila was ready to do it a third time, but the next round of silence ended with only a curt smile from Mademoiselle.

Ms. Rexler nodded them to the back. "Thank you, girls. Can I have numbers forty to forty-nine, please?"

The soft tipping of slippered toes echoed in the room as the next row quickly stepped into place.

Mila eased her way to the floor beside Mo. Mo patted her shoulder.

"You did so good."

"You did, too," Mila said. For the first time the thought of not making it into the program sank into her stomach. "I think we're as good as some of these girls."

Mo nodded firmly and flicked her eyebrow up like *of course*.

Mila pushed herself against the wall as Christol and

Tai stepped into line. She silently wished them both luck and hugged her knees to her chest.

As soon as the music started, Tai's feet went left instead of right.

Come on, Tai, you can do this, Mila rooted in her head, swallowing a gasp. The thought stayed on her heart and near her lips as the music ended.

Mo's arm encircled hers. Mila squeezed it.

"She messed up on that first combination," Mo whispered.

Mila could only nod. Her mouth was too dry to answer.

"She be all right," Mo said. "No cuts till after round two. And next round we do interviews and jazz."

Mila hoped so. One of the judges, a short Black man with a bald head, kept his eye on Tai the entire time like he was assigned to her. He never smiled. Nodded. Winked. Anything. It made Mila nervous.

Mademoiselle Noelle hadn't really looked Tai's way. But she knew Tai, Mila figured. She'd seen her dance before. It was up to the other judges.

The panel made the row perform the combination a total of three times before dismissing them. When Tai plopped down near her, Mila instinctively reached over and touched her arm.

"You did good."

"I guess," Tai said.

The blank look on Tai's face made Mila's stomach feel like dusty, ugly moths were batting their wings inside it. It was the way she felt anytime her and Tai disagreed. The only thing that ever made them go away was going along with Tai.

She reached out to tap Tai, ready to end the stupid feud, but then Christol leaned closer, whispering, "Remember Mademoiselle Noelle said we could use the dance room to rehearse our solos. Wanna practice together?" Her eyes were glossy with excitement. "We can critique each other in case some stuff needs to be fixed." Seeing Mila look over at Tai, Christol added with a smile. "I'll let *you* ask her. But Mo already said she'd be down with it."

"Sounds good," Mila whispered back.

Mila felt like she was standing in the middle of a forked road. One road would get rid of her queasy stomach and make everything between her and Tai okay. The other—she wasn't sure. Practicing dance with Christol and Mo. Helping each other make it into TAG. It felt new and different. She wanted Tai to come down that road with her. But she couldn't make her.

With Christol on one side and Mo on the other, she let herself be pulled into their critiques. Every few seconds one of them would whisper about which girls they thought were good and Mila would pass the comment back and forth. Tai sat quiet, her face stony even when Mo tapped her into the conversation.

Pointing out how many strong dancers were auditioning made Mila nervous, but in a good way. By the end of the day the ugly moths were replaced by excited butterflies.

When they finally stepped outside and onto the buses, Mila was shocked to see daylight. It felt like they'd been in auditions for days. Once back in the Cove she floated down the street, going over the day's combination in her head, humming the music aloud. She raced into the house, yelling hello to her brothers and undressed.

Her phone rang as she headed to the shower.

Cinny.

"Heyyyy," she sang, ecstatic.

"Umph, I was going to ask how your audition went but it musta been good. You sound happy," Cinny said.

Mila shared every detail with Cinny. Minutes later, breathless from her own chatter, she dialed it back to let Cinny talk about whatever she wanted.

"That's so good, Mi," Cinny said, sounding like a proud momma. "So how you and Metai getting along these days?"

It wasn't an odd question coming from Cinny. She'd never cared for Metai. Mila knew it was her own fault for always sharing when Tai got on her nerves. Even when Mila didn't complain, Cinny always checked in to make sure there was no drama between the girls.

Mila cradled the phone closer to her lips, debating how much to share. There was no sense in lying. Cinny would hear it in her voice.

"We not really talking," she admitted.

"It's always something with her. What now?" Cinny asked.

"It's stupid," Mila said.

"It always is," Cinny said. "So what her hot tail mad about now?"

She gave her sister the most basic lowdown, leaving out Tai's comment about her being grimy. Cinny would demand to know why Tai would say something like that about squeaky-clean Mila, of all people.

"I keep telling you to stop messing with Metai, but I know that's easier said than done," Cinny said. Mila could practically see the eye roll. "Real talk, Tai has always been jealous of you. I don't think she even know how to be a friend, because she so busy always wanting what you have."

"Like what?" Mila scowled. "Tai gets whatever she wants from Ms. Sophia. She's the one with more clothes than the store. And her grandmother finally let her cut her hair. What is she jealous about . . . me having to watch Jeremy every day after school or cook dinner three times a week?" A sense of righteous annoyance crept up her neck.

Cinny sucked her teeth. "You always so daggone innocent, Jamila." She laughed like it was cute, but her voice was laced with warning. "Trust, Tai is jealous of you. For a few dozen reasons, probably, but what she hate most is she's a Cove girl and you not. And every single time you do something like wanting to move or liking to take ballet, it reminds her that you not. She hates that."

When she didn't respond, Cinny's voice came loud in her ear. "Know what I'm saying?"

"Yeah," Mila said. She didn't mean it. She heard what

Cinny said and it made some sense. But it had never been this bad between her and Tai. There were good memories. Lots of them. She listened on obediently a few more minutes before begging off to get cleaned up.

In the shower she thought about Cinny's advice. It was the same advice she always gave—don't let Metai get to you; do you.

It was easy for Cinny to tell someone to be themselves. She never had a problem saying exactly how she felt to anyone. And, she didn't have to live right across the street from Tai. She didn't know how it felt to have your best friend look through you like you weren't even there. Mila wanted to make new friends and do new things. But did it have to mean losing Tai?

The water pelted the day's funk from her body and beat an admission out of her. She had been wrong to keep the thing about Roland from Tai, but it was dumb to beef over it. There was no way Tai could disagree with that. Could she?

Mila dressed quickly, the courage from the hot shower still steaming in her.

On the way down the hallway, she peeked her head into JJ and Jeremy's room. It was like an explosion of two worlds. On JJ's side were posters of NFL cheerleaders in tiny shorts and tops that barely held their breasts in. Yellowing newspaper clips from JJ's AAU team wallpapered the areas between the posters. On Jeremy's side were his drawings—stick people at war and play and a family pic that made them look like smiley-faced blob people.

JJ wanted his own room and had even tried to convince their dad Mila should share with Jeremy. A plan that only made sense to him. Which is exactly why he hadn't won the argument.

Mila yelled over JJ's ranting into his headphone.

"I'm heading out."

His eyebrow raised. "'Scuse me? What you think, you me or something? Just dipping out. You feed Nut yet?"

"Whatever, JJ." She walked away then stepped back. "Hey . . ." She waited until he stopped cursing out the person on the other end. "Is Mr. Bryant still out there?"

"Man, hold up. My little sister trying fug my game right now. Son, just hold up." He sighed dramatically, paused the game, and muted his headset. His eyebrow arched higher in case she wasn't aware he was annoyed. When she didn't react, his lanky body relaxed. He snorted smugly. "Yeah he still out there. Why? Ms.

Sophia thinking he clean? She crazy if she do."

"I don't know," she admitted. "But the other day when I was over Tai's he came home high and just started going off because Roland and Simp were there."

He scowled at her. "Was Ms. Sophia home while they was there?"

Mila sucked her teeth. "No. But so what? It's just Roland and Simp."

JJ sat up. His elbows rested on his thighs. The game controller jiggled as he lectured. "Yeah, okay, tell Daddy that." His laugh was short and mean at the fleeting look of concern on her face. "Yeah, that's what I thought. You wouldn't. First of all, Rollie cool and all but he a dough boy."

"JJ, stop. Roland not like that. Don't spread rumors," Mila said, alarmed.

Any other time hearing JJ use the term for *hustlers* would have made her laugh thinking about the time Jeremy had overheard their dad call Rock Jensen a dope boy and thought he'd said "dough." He'd instantly wondered how come he'd never seen Rock selling cookies. It was the one time JJ didn't burst his bubble to explain what it really meant. But if Roland was hustling, it wasn't funny.

JJ's eyebrows formed a deep V as he scolded her back. "Bean, youn know what I know. Trust, him and Simp dough boys."

Mila's mouth laid open. She could barely process what JJ was saying.

He snapped her out of her daze. "Second, you need stop messing with Tai anyway. Her father all messed up. And she gonna end up getting got if she don't slow down."

Head still reeling, she defended Tai. "Tai not like that, JJ. She just a lot of talk."

"Puh," he said with an eye roll. "She hung out at the court nearly every night with Sheeda all up in people's faces including mine. Somebody gonna take her up on all she pretending to offer one day."

His nasty snicker made Mila's face hot. She didn't want to think about Tai out there doing anything with any dude but definitely not with her brother. She lectured back with more force than she felt. "She all talk, JJ. You gonna end up the one with your feelings hurt if you ever try and test all that mouth she have."

JJ leaned back in the chair, his long legs stretching out for days. "Youn need worry about me. I ain't trying rock nobody who's my baby sister's friend." He made a face like he'd tasted something sour. "On top of all that, her father straight cracked out. She cute but she ain't worth that." He turned his back and yelled into the headset. "Look, punk, see what I got for you."

Mila didn't want to believe any of it. There were definitely dough boys their age, even younger. If they were caught they didn't get real jail time. She knew a few dudes who had gone to juvenile detention. They were older now. Some of them graduated to real jail.

JJ was tapped into what went on in their neighborhood, but it didn't mean he was always right. She held on to that tiny hope even as she admitted to herself that he'd been right about at least half of it— Mr. Bryant was obviously high the other day. He was still using drugs.

One thing her and Tai would always have in common—drug addict parents. The only difference was Ms. Sophia kept letting her son back in the house, hoping he'd straighten up. Mila's dad had long ago banished her mother from their home.

She had no solid memories of her mother in the house. She tried to imagine her always in and out, like Mr. Bryant, causing drama whenever she was there, and silently thanked her dad for being the way he was.

Jeremy sat on the sofa eating a bowl of cereal, flicking between five different channels, happy to have the big television to himself. The TV blared, going from commercial to cartoon mania to canned laughter in three seconds.

"Stop switching so much, Nut," Mila chastised. "You gonna give yourself a headache."

He munched, mouth full. "Waa-oooh-owing?"

"Over to my friend Christol's," she said. "I'll be back in an hour."

"Are you cooking?" he asked, hopeful.

She shook her head. "Jeremy, you're eating now. I know this not your first bowl."

He put up two fingers. "But I'mma be hungry in an hour."

"Dinner is up to Daddy. See you," she said, escaping before he could pelt her with dinner suggestions.

She stepped out into the thick air, the heat kissing her shower-cool skin. She crossed the street to Tai's, knocked, waited, and knocked again. She leaned away as the door ripped open.

Tai stood at the door in a pair of cotton shorts and a T-shirt. Her hair was crinkly from the shower.

"Hey," Mila said. Hearing how loud she sounded,

she started again. "Chrissy got permission to use La May to rehearse for the jazz round. Not sure when yet. But want to come?"

"Why would I?" Tai frowned.

Mila chanted in her head: *Be the bigger friend. Be the bigger friend.*

"Just to get out the house," she said. She thought using the line Tai usually used on her would make her laugh. Instead, Tai went in on her.

"Oh, like I'm always telling you and you always—'I don't feel like it. I don't want to,'" Tai said, mocking. "Naw, I'm good." She leaned against the door, arms folded.

Mila pushed her frustration aside with effort. "So how long are we going to keep fighting? I mean, just let me know and then I'll check back when it's good."

She'd sat on the sidelines many times as Tai had treated other people like they were a gnat she wanted to smack. And she'd always sent her apologies to them in her head. Now she was the gnat.

"Who are you anyway?" Tai's eyes scoured Mila's face like she was really trying to identify her. "I don't know no more."

"I'm just trying to dead the drama between us, Tai."

Mila put her palms out, turned them over. "See no tricks. That's it."

"Okay, Bean. My bad . . . I mean Mila or Jamila, whatever you going by these days." Tai's little shoulder shrug was worse than a fake apology. "I get it. Good girls be having a guilty conscience, so you apologizing for the shade. Cool."

"How is me trying to make up a bad thing, Metai? Like, what do you want me to say?" Mila asked. She held Tai's dead-eyed gaze even though she wanted to run and never bother again. With every ounce of energy she had, Mila forced herself to stand her ground. "I didn't throw shade, but if you thought I was the other day or whatever, I'm sorry." She took a breath to gain control. "It's stupid for us to keep arguing, especially over a boy."

Tai laughed a loud "ha." Her eyes beamed into Mila's, not letting go. "This not even really about Rollie since it's me he like anyway." Her shoulders shrugged hard. "But for real, I'm tired of being the ghetto chick while you pretend to play the goodie-good bougie girl. Period. That act been old."

For as long as Mila could remember, she and Tai had been connected like some Siamese twin experiment gone bad. And all summer, she had finally felt like they'd been separated enough so she could think her own thoughts. Walking out of Tai's face should have been easy. Yet all Mila wanted to do was apologize, for everything—for not telling her about talking to Roland, for not being able to get that day out of her head, for the sun being yellow if that would just end it.

Because the thought of them living across the street from each other and never uttering another word set a new flock of moths loose in her belly. She couldn't do it. They couldn't be enemies. Even if it meant begging Tai to let this go and go back to how they had always been. The apology was on the tip of her tongue, then Tai's rant changed everything.

"What's messed up is, you keep wanting everybody to think you so above it. Like you don't have no secrets."

"I should have told you I saw Rollie this summer. I just—" Mila said before Tai cut her off.

"Oh my God, please. If you wanted to tell me, you would have." The smirk on her face took Mila's breath away. She felt gut-punched as Tai added, "Girl, bye."

Mila's will to fight for their friendship was in the wind, instantly, leaving her deflated.

She stumbled home with the finality of Tai's last

words whispering in her ears, for hours, forcing her to lie about having cramps—the only way in a house full of boys that ever got her time to herself.

Her and Tai were officially no longer friends. She laid in bed, draped in two big blankets, shivering, thinking about it until sleep took mercy on her and quieted her mind.

CHAPTER
14

Nona was big on breakfast.

Tai usually liked their mandatory morning meal. But this time Nona was on one, going on and on. It was like Nona sat and took notes on everything, even stuff Tai didn't think she was paying attention to. Today it was how come Mila hadn't been around?

Tai would have bet her life that normally her answer, "I don't know, Nona, you know Mila half nerd always wanting be by herself," would have shut down any more questions. But no, Nona put her coffee cup down and folded her arms. Her brown eyes pierced Tai's long enough to make her squirm. When Tai offered no more explanation, Nona's lips pressed together, then opened with a small pop as she sighed.

All Tai could think was, *Here we go.* She stared into her half-eaten bowl of cereal as Nona asked, "What's going on, Metai?" like she'd already decided something was wrong and Tai was at fault.

Tai pushed the soggy bowl of cereal back and made the mistake of folding her own arms and glaring back.

Nona was up, like a whip, sending her chair skittering back a few inches. She pulled herself up to her full five feet and got that look on her face that threatened a beating that never came but always promised to.

"Unah, don't you dare look at me like you trying to challenge me, girl. I had to watch your sad butt walk around this house grumbling like you ain't have no other friends around here while Bean was gone. Now she back home and y'all barely seen each other . . . what's up?"

Tai's arms dropped limp to her side fast. She wanted to come clean. To ask Nona why people changed? And, the one question that had really been on her mind the last few days, *how* could people change? Because a part of her wanted to be whatever kind of friend Bean seemed to be looking for.

It hurt to admit that she wasn't a good enough friend anymore. Bean had never really fit in, in their hood, always so quiet in the middle of how loud the Cove was. But now it was like Bean finally realized that. Worse, this sudden knowledge seemed like it was a light beaming on every flaw Tai had.

Tai knew she wasn't perfect. Yeah, she could be bossy. But in the Cove it was boss or be bossed.

She was seconds from confessing it all to Nona until her grandmother turned around and said, "What did you do, Metai? Is Bean mad at you because you finally hurt her feelings enough to make her stand up for herself?"

Tai's mouth pinched into a stubborn pout. If Nona was gonna assume, there was no point in going into the whole mess.

Nona was by her chair in two steps, her hands around Tai's shoulder, rubbing.

"I didn't mean to hurt your feelings, baby girl." She squatted easily beside Tai's chair. "I know you can't help always being so . . . tough on the outside. But I see how you always beaugard Jamila. Even the best of friends gotta learn when enough is enough, Metai. I thought maybe y'all being apart all summer would make you appreciate how good a friend she is and help you tone it down a little."

"Why you assume I did something, Nona?" Tai asked, finally letting tears flow hot and hard.

Nona nodded. "You're right. That was wrong of me." She pushed herself up and pulled her chair over so she was at Tai's side. The smell of her soap mingled between them, making Tai want to lie in her arms, but she stayed upright rigid. Angry at Nona, Bean, and herself.

"Do you want to share what happened?" Nona asked. "Because I'm not stupid. Something not right."

"I really don't feel like talking about it," Tai said. She wiped her face and dared folding her arms again. "Me and Bean fine." Her sigh was heavy. "I mean, me and Jamila fine. That's what she want to be called now."

Seeing Tai's side eye at her chuckling, Nona stroked her hair in apology. "What's so wrong with her growing out of a nickname, Metai? Y'all be in high school soon."

"Nothing," Tai said. She wasn't in the mood to explain it all. "Like I said, we fine. She just all into this new girl, Christol. I'm not feeling the girl so—" She shrugged with force. "We not chilling as much. That's all."

Tai's phone chimed four times, her tone for Mini Chat with Sheeda, Bean, and Mo. "That's her now."

Her heart leaped, hopeful. "See. We cool. Can I go?"

Nona eyed the phone. A smile lurked behind her doubt that everything was suddenly good. Tai forced it all the way out by shining the phone screen at Nona. The words *My girls* ran across the bar alerting her she had a message.

"Go ahead." Nona's head shook. "I swear I'm too old to be dealing with this kind of drama."

Tai couldn't resist teasing. "So next time I call you old, don't get mad then."

Nona's laugh was rich in the quiet morning. "Your fast butt make me feel old." She wiggled her hips. "But make no mistake, Nona fit and forty."

"Forty-five," Tai corrected before racing away from the towel Nona swatted at her.

Nona switched sides about her age every other day. Either she was too old to be doing this or that or she was fussing about not being old enough to be doing this or that. It depended on the situation, but both declarations usually came whenever she had to step in and be the mother and grandmother for Tai.

Tai raced up the stairs, leaving her grandmother muttering good-naturedly about having to clear up the dishes. The phone sounded again and again as others jumped into the chat. She sailed onto her bed, sat cross-legged, and scrolled the messages fast, looking to see what Bean had said. But it was only Mo and Sheeda.

Mo'Betta: *2nd day of auditions leggo!!! im siced and don't care who know it especially since we on jazz and I can shake my 🚫 lololol*

She-da-Man: *the drama audition was pretty cool. Im tired as shankypook. Wuz up all nite memorizing that spoken word thing I did at church 2 years ago. I think I was saying it in my sleep Lolz*

Mo'Betta: *omg I remember dat. U went HAM on that Maya Angelou and the church lost they minds. I had almost forgot*

She-da-Man: *yeah like itz the only thing I could get together. I didn't know we was supposed to prepare a piece. Nervous!! Where everybody at? Hello Mila? Umm Tai?*

Mo'Betta: *u gon tear it up. U got today and long as u don't go first u got time to keep rehearsing tomorrow. Idk where these chicks at. But I hope they done made up by now 😌 lololol*

At seeing her name, Tai reluctantly entered the fray.

DatGirlTai: *for yall information if we just talking bout TAG I'm ready be out. 👟*

She-da-Man: *u so common. Always shading somebodys*

shine. Lolz Mo said ur audition went good yesterday. Whut u scurred bro? 😂 😂 😂

A grin wormed its way across Tai's face. If Mo thought Tai did good, that had to mean something. She wasn't about to let on she cared, though.

DatGirlTai: *Ain't nobody scared. just not all pressed like yall. #Noshade*

Mo'Betta: *y put urself through it though for real?*

She-da-Man: *cuz rollie got that azz open and she trying keep her eye on him b4 one of these county girls get him*

Tai laughed out loud. Sheeda was closer to the truth than she probably knew.

DatGirlTai: *W/e Sheeda. Oun think Rollie into bougie girls. No worries.* 💀

Mo'Betta: *SMH where Bean?*

Tai refused to answer even though she knew the question was for her.

She-da-Man: *wow crickets lolz*

Mo'Betta: *OMG are yall for real still beefing? Like I can't. I just can't. smh*

DatGirlTai: *Calm down mother goose. My God*

She-da-Man: *Are ya'll still beefing tho?*

DatGirlTai: *Jus cuz I didn't answer where she at? W/e yall. She not here w/me so idk jus like ya'll. Ain't no beef*

Mo'Betta: *Well did ya'll make up?*

Tai couldn't bring herself to tell them that she'd only made things worse.

When Bean had showed up the other day, she had been all ready to apologize for going off about the Rollie thing. She really had. Then Bean had bucked up and it scared Tai how different she was. Her mouth had spewed before her mind could stop it. The memory of Bean's eyes widening then falling heavy made her feel sick.

Secretly she hoped Bean would jump into the chat and say something. If she did, Tai would make it right. Squash it 100 percent.

After a few minutes, Mo hit back with *??????*

Tai almost sent her own question marks back. Instead, she dropped the phone on the bed and left them hanging. She forced herself to get to work. In a few days it would be time for school shopping. Before that could happen, she had to know what items she wanted and needed—the easy part—and she had to give away a "significant" amount of old clothes to get new ones. Nona's rule was to have giveaway clothes packed before she announced it was time to go shopping. If Tai didn't, the shopping spree was off. The trick was Nona never set exactly when shopping time would be.

Tai had tested this once. Fifth grade when Nona announced, "Time to go school shopping"—purse on her arm meaning at that moment—and saw Tai hadn't bagged up any giveaway clothes, she went right back downstairs, turned on the TV, and ignored Tai's promise that it would only take ten minutes to get the clothes together.

They had gone shopping the very next weekend instead. But it was one of the few times Tai hadn't blustered or cried her grandmother into letting her have her way.

She grabbed her laptop and signed into Skyvo in case Rollie logged on, then pulled every item out of her closet. Minutes later she earned a few brownie points when Nona stuck her head in, before leaving for work, saw Tai surrounded by a mountain of clothes, and winked.

With the house empty, she turned on music. The rapid-fire chatter of the hip-hop made the house feel full. Quiet when Nona was home was different than when she was gone. Tai hated the alone quiet.

Even through the low thump of the bass, she heard her phone buzzing. She wasn't ready to face a screen full of messages with none from Bean. Every time it went off, she forced herself to grab an item of clothing and decide its fate—keep or donate. Bean had to jump in at some point. It wasn't like she was beefing with Mo and Sheeda. Once she did, Tai vowed she'd check the vibe, then find a way to dead the argument between them.

Forty-five minutes later she was enjoying the seasonal purge more than she expected to. Bonus, she'd found Bean's *Me Too* T-shirt. Tai had the shirt's fraternal twin that said *I'm Hot*. They only ever wore them together and were supposed to wear them on the last day of school but Bean hadn't been able to find it. No wonder. It had been buried on the bottom of the closet. She tossed it, aiming for the bed. It clung to the side of her mattress like a rock climber struggling to make it to the top.

Soon she was in her own little fort surrounded by three large trash bags of giveaways. Other clothes, more than she realized she had, piled like snowdrifts around her. She bopped her head, singing along under her breath.

Her father called from downstairs. "Ay . . . ay, who home?"

Tai ignored him.

After a few seconds of sounding like a parrot who only knew one phrase, he finally made his way up the stairs. Tai catapulted herself off the floor and onto her bed. Her father stationed himself just outside the room like an invisible shield kept him from going further.

She lay on her stomach, her back to the door, phone in hand, still pretending not to hear him. She gasped when she saw that Bean had finally joined the chat. She skimmed, trying to get to the beginning of the message.

"Shoot," she muttered, fighting the phone's sensitive screen as it seesawed between that morning's chat and the end of the current chat. The words were a jumble, but she caught enough to know the girls were trying to make some moves later that included the guys. Forcing her fingers to behave, she swiped slow and deliberate, trying to hit the start of the latest chat.

Her father's voice boomed louder than it needed to. "Tai, I know you heard me calling you."

"No, you yelled 'Ay.' That's not the same as calling me," she said, without turning.

Finally, the top of the chat came into focus. She got as far as Mo's message saying,

Hey Chrissy texted me. Look like her place . . . before

her father's yammering forced her to sit up and talk to him. He'd stand there forever just to annoy her if she didn't. He was childish like that.

He asked a million questions he should have known the answer to: What time did Nona get off from work? Was anybody cooking? Did his check get mailed here?

"Nona's schedule been the same for like . . ." She squinted at the wall, pretending she was really trying to pick a precise date before settling on "a million years. How do you not know she work eleven to seven every day? Unless she working overtime."

"Well, is she working late tonight?" he asked, hands slouched in his pocket, satisfied that he was getting some answers.

"Hold up, let me look." Tai picked up her phone, scrolled. She cocked her head in more mock thought before shrugging. "Sorry. According to my schedule, today wasn't my day to keep track of her."

The look of burnt stupidity on her father's face filled her with giddy satisfaction.

"Why your mouth so smart?" he asked, nearly pouting.

"Why you coming to me to ask where *your* mother is?" she shot back, wanting to add, *I'm the child*, but she knew it wouldn't matter. She was thirteen and he was twenty-eight, but her father was young-minded—one step up from Simp as far as she was concerned.

He ran his tongue over his teeth. The habit disgusted Tai. It looked so nasty. But it also meant he didn't have a comeback. A tiny smile crept across her lips. "You lucky I don't believe in beatings," he said, mean-mugging unsuccessfully.

Tai's eyes rolled. She dropped the phone back onto the bed and went back to folding clothes between the giant trash bags. Her ignoring him wasn't enough. He remained in her doorway. She looked up at him and directed him like she really was the parent. "Just call Nona and ask her if she working late, Dad-dy."

She broke the word up, like saying it offended her tongue too much to let it roll naturally.

"That's right, 'bout time you remember I'm the parent," he said, grinning like he'd really won something. Then just as quickly he went back to worrying. "But I already did call her. She ain't answer." He cocked his elbow on the door sill and stared out Tai's window, pondering his options. "I need my check, man. I wonder if she put it away."

"Just text her and ask if she put it away . . . goodness,"

she said, openly disgusted at having to direct him through such a simple problem.

"Metai, I'm your father. You need to be a better daughter and respect me." He folded his arms, thumbs stuck out from his pits, looking down at her over the mountainous bags.

Tai had a long list of reasons she didn't respect her father. But she found herself calm, for once. "I will when you act like a father," she said, without a hint of sarcasm. They'd had this conversation before and she was over it.

He glared at her, hurt in his eyes. "Man, whatever," he said.

For a few seconds they eyeballed one another, both waiting for the next shot. Tai had nothing else to say. To break up the standoff she got up, snatched her phone off the bed, and plopped back on the floor to read the chat. Eventually he walked away. By the time he did, Tai had the full story. Chrissy and her brother had invited everybody to chill at their spot. Everybody was going—Rollie, Simp, Sheeda, Mo, and even Bean.

Even Bean.

CHAPTER
15

When Mila got the text from Chrissy saying her and Chris could have company as long as they all stayed outside, Mila was quick to apologize for ditching their plans the day before. She'd been ready for drama. To her relief, Chrissy had shrugged it off. Said she had ended up falling asleep on the couch anyway.

It was new having her apology accepted without shaming or a cold shoulder. She accepted Chrissy's invitation even when she saw later that Tai also agreed to come through.

She gave herself a pep talk as her noodles cooled.

This was just the way it was now. Her and Tai were over.

Hurt zagged down her chest, the pain raw like a scraped knee.

JJ wandered into the kitchen, bleary-eyed. "Why you be getting up so early? Making all that noise cooking."

"It's eleven o'clock. That's not early," she said, blowing softly over the noodles. Steam spiraled from the bowl as JJ grabbed her fork, dug into the bowl, and stuffed a mouthful of noodles into his mouth.

"JJ!" she exclaimed.

He huffed from the hot pasta, noodles hanging out of his mouth. He scarfed down a few then spit the rest in the sink.

"That's what you get," she said, shaking her head. "You all right?"

"Man, those things are blazing," he said between gulps of water.

"If you asked I would have shared the bowl," she said, only mildly annoyed. "Hey, have you hung out with Chris, the new dude, yet?"

JJ leaned against the sink, the cool glass against his burned tongue. He lisped as he talked. "Christh . . . the twin? Yeah, I met him." He stroked his lip with his thumb, smiling. "His sister got them thickum thighs."

"Um-ew." Mila frowned. "Remember, you don't like messing with my friends. So let me warn you, me and Chrissy are friends now."

"I don't mess with none of your *old* friends. Thickum is fair game," he said with a snicker. "Chris seem like cool peoples though. I balled with him a few times. Why?"

"I'm going over there today. . . ." Seeing his narrow-eyed suspicion she added quickly, "His sister invited me."

"Don't let me find out y'all over there 'experimenting.'"

Mila rolled her eyes. "I just met the boy, JJ. You always gotta go there."

"Who else coming?" he asked.

"Oh, you're playing big brother today?"

He folded his arms. "I'm always big brother. So who coming?"

"Roland, Simp, the girls," Mila said.

His mouth turned up in disapproval. "I told you be careful about hanging with Rollie and Simp."

"Are you sure they work with Angel?" She heard the plea in her voice but couldn't shake it. Angel was the best friend of Cinny's boyfriend, Raheem. Everyone knew he hustled. But Raheem didn't and they'd been friends forever. She held out hope that Rollie was only guilty for being around the wrong people or something. "I've never seen them hand off anything."

JJ kept leaning against the sink, his legs crossed at his feet, casually schooling her. "Ouno all the details. I'm not in their business like that. But I know what I heard and they definitely in the game somehow."

"But Roland's a nice person." It sounded childish to Mila's ears but it was all she had. "And Simp acts so slow sometimes, I can't see anybody trusting him to deal."

JJ shot down her arguments. "Real talk, I told you Rollie all right with me. Ouno how 'nice' he is, but Angel a good dude, too, ain't he? And he deal."

He raised his arms like *Well?*

He had a point. Angel looked, dressed, and acted like any other sixteen-year-old. But he was also Martinez's nephew. Most everyone knew he was in the game, no matter how hard he tried to hide it.

The only person Mila knew for sure looked like a dealer was Rock and that was because of how many times she'd seen him on the corner exchanging drugs for money.

It depressed her that she couldn't prove JJ wrong.

He kept piling on proof. "Shoot, you ever seen Rollie in a pair of busted kicks?"

Mila dismissed it. "A lot of people dress nice but not dough boys, Jay."

He nodded. "Yeah. But Rollie and Simp stay laced in new basketball shoes."

"I mean I thought they got 'em from being on the Marauders."

JJ grinned.

"Exactly. Most of the dudes on the team wrapped up in the game. Why you think Daddy ain't never let me play for 'em?"

Mila's mouth gaped. She had never thought about it. Her dad had a lot of rules. She only focused on the ones that applied to her.

"Look, I don't think they deep in it," JJ said with surprising kindness. "I thought you knew, for real. Just watch yourself when you around 'em in case dumb mess pop off. All right?"

She was numb from the information. But now she had a feeling she knew what Simp had been talking about over Tai's that day—"We'll miss you on the block," he had said. Goose bumps peppered her arms.

His kind moment gone, JJ scowled at her as he lectured. "Yeah, and keep your legs closed. Leave these hardheads round here alone."

"That's disgusting," Mila said vehemently, desperate to hide her embarrassment.

"That's big brother advice," he said, then rolled out of the kitchen.

Mila left the bowl of uneaten noodles in the middle of the table with a note to Jeremy that he could heat them up in the microwave if he wanted. She thought about hiding them so JJ wouldn't eat them first. But Jeremy had to start fending for himself.

She hollered out, to nobody in particular, that she was gone and went to step out the door.

There was a bundle of cloth on the step. She picked it up and shook it. It was her *Me Too* T-shirt.

She looked over at Tai's then down the street. If Tai had just dropped it, she had haul-tailed away. Mila stared down at the lost shirt like it could tell her how it landed there. She laid it on the table near the door and walked on, her throat tight.

Kids streamed out of houses like ants anxious to be outside of their underground caves. They sat in small groups on front stoops or side yards, hung at the rec center, or surrounded the basketball court. In two weeks the rhythm would change drastically. For her it already had. Since the TAG auditions it seemed like the girls, Rollie, Simp, and even the twins were officially a crew. It sank in once Mila saw everyone together in the twins' backyard.

Yard was a generous term for it. A tall person could take ten steps to the back and ten steps to the left or right before hitting the fence that separated it from the neighbors'. The twins' mother had stuffed as much in the space as she could.

Tai, Roland, Chris, and Simp were at a small round table in the middle of the yard. A large brown and beige striped umbrella shaded it from the sun's beam. Four chairs strapped with soft plastic bands surrounded it.

Mila wasn't surprised Tai was sitting at the table with the guys rather than the girls. They were probably the only reason she had come. She sat between Chris and Roland, her body leaned into Roland as she commented on something he'd said.

Mila joined Sheeda, Mo, and Chrissy around what Mila immediately named the nook. It was a cozy spot with a small wicker love seat and two full round wicker chairs up against the house. A big empty copper bowl sat in the middle of the furniture. Mila only knew it was a fire pit because one of Aunt Jacqs' neighbors had them over one night and they'd made s'mores over one.

She stared at the far back corner at four huge rocks big enough to sit on but also random and sort of out of place.

Chrissy laughed. "I know, right. Those rocks are ginormous."

"They really are," Mila said.

"It's a flower bed," Chrissy said, pointing to the tiny colorful buds only visible when you walked right up to the rocks. "It's the first time we not living in an apartment, so my mother went HAM on this yard."

"Just a little bit," Mila said. She laughed along, liking that Chrissy didn't seem embarrassed.

Once you added people, there really was too much in the yard. But Mila liked that Ms. Mason had decorated. Her own yard had an old picnic table that gave you splinters and two big plastic bins where her dad stored tools and other boy junk. None of them really used the yard.

She felt Tai's eyes on her. So far they hadn't said a word to each other and no one had questioned what was up. She was sure Mo would ask later. But Cove code was simple—in public leave people's beef between them. Mila found herself thankful for the neighborhood's stupid little rules for once. She bunched her knees to her chest to escape the sun creeping its way closer to the nook.

Most of the conversation centered on whose muscles were the sorest and Sheeda being a little jealous that she couldn't take part in the moaning. It took Mila's mind off Tai's coolness.

"Do you think everybody gonna make TAG?" Sheeda asked. She slapped on a pair of oval shades that made her look like a fashionable owl.

"For real, I've been wondering the same thing," Mo said. She leaned up in the chair, elbows on her thighs. "Part of me says it's impossible because of how many people were there. But . . . then again we tight with Mademoiselle. So . . ."

Chrissy scooted to the edge of the love seat. "I was talking to one of the people at the photo station. She said there were two hundred fifty people signed up." Her mouth twisted and her eyebrows went up before she exhaled and dashed their hopes. "I think the program can only hold one fifty."

"They cutting a hundred people?" Sheeda asked in

dismay. "I can't see me making it then. Most of the people trying out for drama been in all these plays and stuff since they were like five or whatever." She sat back cross-legged in her chair, deep in thought.

"You never know," Mila said, because it felt like the right thing to say. Doubt shrouded the confidence she'd felt the other day.

Mo's head shook vigorously. "Wait. That means they only picking thirty people for each discipline?"

"Right," Chrissy said. She sat back and folded her legs beneath her. Her feet pressed up against Mila's own bare feet. The contact reassured Mila. Even with the fear growing, she found herself comforted that everyone was nervous.

Mo's lip stretched out as she puffed out an exaggerated breath. "That's a lot of cutting." She brightened. "I still feel like us knowing Mademoiselle will make a difference. She gotta hook up the La May girls."

She looked to Mila for reassurance.

"If she has a vote I think she'll fight for any La May girl," Mila said. She didn't really believe the other judges could be told what to do that easily. But Mo's entire face lit up, making the lie worth it.

"That's what I'm saying," Mo said.

"What you saying about what?" Tai asked, suddenly there standing between the love seat and Mo's chair. She stayed focused on Mo, never looking Mila's way.

Mila played along. This was what it was going to be like.

"Bean was saying that she think Mademoiselle would fight to get her students in the program," Mo said confidently.

Tai's eyes rolled in Mila's direction. "Hmph, maybe she'd fight for her. But if she not the one making the final decision, I don't see what difference it's gonna make if the other judges disagree."

It surprised Mila that she and Tai were on the same page. But she kept mum. Saying anything would probably just open the door for more drama. She was glad when the guys came over to fill the silence between them.

Chris and Roland stood behind the love seat. Simp placed himself behind Tai. She immediately took a step away, squashing herself against the love seat and Roland.

"What y'all doing?" Simp asked.

"Getting their feelings hurt," Tai said.

"Really, Tai?" Mo asked, scowling. "Chill. Just a little. Please."

"It just got real," Sheeda said. She threw her hands up. "I really can't see me making it. But good luck, I guess."

"Y'all just realizing how competitive it is?" Chris asked. He frowned at the silence, then tapped a beat in the air as he talked. "No sense being scared now, though."

Roland's face, curious when he'd walked over, was serious like he was thinking on it.

The circle was quiet until Tai, with a shrug in her voice, declared, "That's why I don't know why y'all was so siced, in the first place. Everybody and their brother in the county trying out."

"I ain't trying be ignorant, but ain't like none of y'all gonna be superstars," Simp said. He had to raise his voice over the protests and chorus of "Shut up, Simp." "Real talk, they asking people audition. So don't that mean they tryna pick the best?" His brown eyes wandered the circle, waiting for somebody to argue. "I'm just saying, I bet some of those girls trying out was in them pink tutu things when they was babies."

Roland and Chris laughed under their breath. Tai flicked an eyebrow at Roland.

"Naw, I was laughing at him saying pink tutu

things," he explained, a smile playing on his lips.

Tai rolled her eyes at him. Still Mila felt replaced. Tai seemed fine pretending that she wasn't there. She forced herself to go along.

"I don't think nobody need wild out about it," Chris said. He sat on the back of the love seat. Everybody was looking their way, waiting on any wisdom or hope. "They gonna pick the best, for sure. But they gonna pick some ones they can mold, too."

Mila felt relief fall over the group like sun rays hiding behind a cloud.

"They did say that," Sheeda said, nodding, eager to believe.

Tai spoke up. "Yeah, well it didn't seem like a lot of girls in dance gonna fall into the non-talented group."

Chris smiled. "I didn't say some people ain't have no talent."

Their laughter quieted when Simp barged in with, "I don't care what y'all say. I think this stuff be rigged."

"Why would they go through all this if they already knew who they wanted?" Mila asked. She chided him softly, "Everybody not just out to game people, Simp."

There was some hurt on his face but he only shrugged.

Mo jumped in, quick to agree. "They could have just made it an invitation-only program if they knew who they wanted. You just mad 'cause you can't try out yet."

His face tightened. "Forget you, Mo. Ain't nobody pressed 'cept you."

"At least I *can* be pressed," Mo said.

"Come on y'all, don't argue," Mila said.

She begged Mo with her eyes, anxious to keep the peace.

Mo had three older brothers. All but the youngest was in jail. She knew how to give as good as she got and rarely backed down. And as mild-mannered as Simp was most of the time, he could handle himself. And knowing that he might be (was?) a dough boy made Mila look at him differently now. Before, she wouldn't have worried about him and Mo dissing each other. But now? Who knew what might set Simp off if everybody kept teasing him about not being able to do TAG?

"I'm not pressed one bit," Tai said, breaking the tension. It was as close to siding with Simp as she would ever get. He looked at her with open adoration. "But if I can make it and get out of art or gym a few times a week, shoot, might as well."

There were a few halfhearted "Yeahs" from the group. But the conversation had cooled the high they'd all been on after the first day.

Roland put his fist out to Chris. They touched knuckles then swiped their hands quickly. "I need rehearse my solo. I check y'all later."

"Can you walk me home first," Tai said, following close behind.

Simp rolled out with them, the third wheel. Mo and Sheeda left shortly after.

"You ready roll, too?" Chrissy asked Mila.

Mila was happy to hear sadness in the question.

Chris took Mo's place in the round chairs. His arms splayed around the back of it. He turned it an inch to the left then right, swiveling softly.

"No shade, but everybody going practice like it's gon' do something now," he said. "Either you ready for this or you not."

His eyes fixed on Mila, like he was trying to figure out which one she was.

She wasn't sure herself. Simp was right. She'd only been dancing a minute. She was competing against other girls like Christol with more experience. She had only really cared about making it into TAG once auditions started. It seemed stupid to be nervous now. Except she was.

"I don't know if I'm one of the talented or the non-talented," she said, meaning it. "But like Chrissy said, I'm ready to work either way. So . . ." She shrugged, as if apologizing for not having a straight answer.

Chrissy gave Mila's knee a congratulatory jiggle. She was grinning crazy. "Then you ready. Right Chris?"

They watched as his chair swiveled to a beat—first to the right, then a tiny double swivel to the left before swinging back. His head nodded along and his lips moved silently until he realized they were both gaping at him.

"Huh?" he asked.

Chrissy rolled her eyes. "He get like that. Just start rhyming all randomly to his self." She jiggled Mina's knee again. "You ready. We both are. We gon' kill the next round of auditions."

"I hope so," Mila said.

She let Chrissy rattle on. Every few minutes she stole a glance at Chris, lost in his own world, lips moving without a sound coming out. They didn't look a thing alike, but they both had the same fire in them. It wasn't just how focused they were on singing and dancing. She knew plenty of people in the Cove who had sang at church and planned to be a chart-topping R&B artist or who balled pretty good and was going to the NBA "one day." Most of them were still in the Cove either still talking about their dream or reminiscing about it.

Chrissy and Chris did more than talk. They were about it.

She vowed to do the same.

CHAPTER
16

Tai pushed her spoon deep into the bowl. The sludge of oatmeal slowly glommed over the sides as it sank. She wiggled the spoon, trying to free it, but Nona's oatmeal was extra thick today. The spoon stayed wedged. It's how she felt—stuck.

It was the last audition day. Jazz and interviews. Instead of being excited she felt dizzy, like everything was moving too fast.

Rollie was feeling her. They talked every day now. She had no doubt that before school started he'd make them exclusive. And if he didn't, well, she was working up her nerve to bring it up.

Her last year at Woodbury Middle and she was going in with a boyfriend. She should have been bouncing off the walls. Instead, she felt more alone than ever.

She picked up her phone and scrolled to Bean's number. All she had to say was *sorry* or something close to it and Bean would forgive her. Probably. The contact floated in front of her eyes. The icons to text or call whispered to her to choose one of them. Her finger hovered over the call button. She snatched it away. She'd just stumble and stutter through a phone call.

She put her finger on the yellow envelope.

Just text her she told herself.

Then she thought about how new girl and Bean had strutted across the yard looking over the big-A rocks in the back. Their laughter had slammed into Tai's head like a hammer. She'd forced herself into the boys' conversation, trying to block the sound.

She clenched her jaw thinking about how easily they had become friends, like Bean had just been waiting for somebody else to kick it with.

Before she could change her mind, she scrolled to the little trashcan in the corner of the contact then hit *yes* to "Are you sure you want to delete?" until all evidence of her friendship with Jamila "Bean" Phillips evaporated. An ache grew in her throat. She swallowed hard, refusing to let a tear lump take over.

Her appetite gone, she dumped her oatmeal into the sink and called out halfheartedly to her grandmother, "Nona, I have to go."

They nearly bumped into each other.

"I'm sorry, baby girl," Nona said. Her eyes widened. "Oh my Lord, you put your bowl in the sink without me asking you to." She put her hand up against Tai's forehead. "You feeling okay?"

Tai nodded woodenly. She knew it was a joke but she couldn't force a laugh.

Nona frowned. "What's wrong? Nervous?"

Tai took the way out. "Yeah. It just seems like I'm wasting my time doing this."

Nona's hand flew to her hips. "Metai Johnson. From the day you were born you've managed to get your way. Whether it was using those big lungs of yours to cry your way to an early bottle feeding." She chucked Tai's chin. "Or when you convinced Ms. White to let y'all kids have two arts and crafts sessions during camp instead of one. You're resourceful when you want to be." She held Tai's chin up so they were eye to eye. "So just want to be today."

She kissed Tai's forehead. It felt so good, Tai wrapped her arms around her grandmother and held on tight while Nona rubbed her head.

"Is there something else wrong?" she asked.

Tai shook her head yes. The tears poured from her eyes.

"What is it?" Nona whispered.

Tai's voice hitched, breaking the words up in a mess of hiccups. "Me—and Bean . . . we not talking." She squeezed her grandmother tighter. "She like . . . she like the new girl better than me. I thought we was girls but . . . but she act like she can't stand me."

"I'm sure that's not the case, baby," Nona said, so gentle and wise Tai wanted to believe her. Their bodies rocked slowly as Nona tried to soothe her. "You're so used to having Jamila to yourself, I don't doubt it's hard to share her. But you know what?" She waited until Tai lifted her head to look at her. "Around here, the more friends you have the better."

Tai buried her head back in Nona's chest. It felt good there.

"So is it that the new girl doesn't like you?" Nona asked, her voice probing.

Tai knew that voice. There was a time when she'd seen her grandmother confront neighborhood kids for picking on Tai and calling her slanty eyes. And if she didn't get the answer she expected, she'd go at their parents. Nona wasn't a pushover. It would have been easy to blame it all on Christol and have Nona step to the girl's mother. Instead, she found herself telling the truth.

"No, she's all right. I was over her house yesterday."

"Well, see," Nona said cheerfully. Her hands rubbed Tai's hair, stroking the short side. "You just have to find a way to be friends with both of them. I'm sure Jamila doesn't mind sharing you. You just have to share her."

"If I don't make it into TAG and they both do, it won't matter anyway," Tai said. Her tears burned off. Some of the original anger simmered under her words.

"Why's that?" Nona asked.

Tai shrugged. "They'll have classes together and stuff."

"Well how 'bout you deal with one problem at a time," Nona said. She gently pried Tai away from her, holding her by the shoulders. "Do your best today at the audition and then give the new friendship a chance."

She saw in Nona's eyes that in her mind this was already fixed. She let her believe it.

"Okay," Tai said. She swiped at her eyes, her mind wandering to where her sunglasses were. All she needed was for everyone to know she'd been crying.

"I have a surprise for you in the living room." Nona pecked her on the cheek. "Break a leg today. You got this."

Tai repeated those words to herself as she put on the gift from Nona—the strappy black leotard with the lace in back, the one she'd wanted since last year—and the entire way there and as she sat in the hallway next to three other girls, waiting to be called in for her interview.

You got this.

You got this.

You have to have this!

CHAPTER
17

The Players Cultural Arts Center was a lot like the city it called home, bigger than it seemed and more sophisticated than it had any right to be. The maze of music and dance rooms and studios gave the place a sense of organized chaos.

Mila hadn't known how huge the center was until she realized she was lost. She slowed her steps and mentally went over the directions again. Leave the auditorium, take a right, hit the second bay of stairs, and go up one flight. Or was she supposed to hit the first bay of stairs and go up two flights?

People glided by. Everyone seemed to know where they were going except her.

She had hoped the dancers would be kept together. There was some comfort in being among the large group even if they were competing with each other. To make it worse, she wasn't with any of her friends. Mo's interview was downstairs. Chrissy's was on something called the mezzanine. Sheeda got to stay in the auditorium and Tai . . . she didn't know. She wasn't going to think about Tai today. This was her last chance to make good on her promise to focus on dance. Not just say it. Really be focused.

The halls brimmed with students. It was hard to tell which was a music room versus a dance room unless you pushed your face up to the long, narrow glass that allowed you only a peek. Worse, the rooms had only a small number beside them in a white glossy plastic that blended into the light oak of the door.

She was looking for Room 234.

It hit her. Second floor. She was at least on the right floor.

Get it together, she told herself. Scared of looking as lost as she felt, she glanced at the number of the door next to her, catching it right as she passed by.

260. She'd gone too far.

She stooped down, pretending to need something out of her bag, rummaged through it for a few seconds, got up, and reversed directions. She peered at the number on the door to make sure she'd gotten it right this time. There were two other girls sitting on the floor outside.

"Looking for two thirty-four?" one girl asked.

Mila felt like hugging her. She nodded then spoke, "Yes," to help herself breathe normal.

The girl patted the floor beside her. "This is it."

Mila's unsteady legs easily led her down to the floor.

"I'm Jenna." Her eyes took Mila in. "I like your leo."

The one thing Mila liked about jazz was being able to wear any color leotard she wanted. She only had three colored ones. She'd picked her favorite, light blue with crisscross straps and lace in the front.

"Jamila," Mila said, glad to stretch her legs out. She prayed they'd steady before she had to dance. "Thanks. Yours is cute, too."

"I'm Lourdes," said the other girl, a ginger with fake eyelashes.

"So this is it," Jenna said. Her eyes were large behind a pair of glasses. They blinked at Mila and

Lourdes expectantly. Mila was too nervous to carry on a full conversation. But one of her fears had been that the other dancers would be snobby. Thank God they weren't. Her nerves couldn't take it.

"Yeah. I'll be glad when it's over," she said.

"I heard that the interview counts for more than the dance audition," Lourdes said, her lashes batting furiously as she looked from Mila to Jenna.

It seemed everybody was desperately pulling pieces together, trying to understand what they'd gotten themselves into. Mila was glad she wasn't the only one. She added what little she knew to the conversation.

"I keep hearing that passion and heart mean a lot to the judges." She exhaled deeply, then smiled as confidently as she could. "We just have to go full out."

Jenna giggled. "You sound like my dance teacher."

"It's 'cause they're all the same," Lourdes said, grinning.

The door opened a peep. An older gentleman, tall and thin, peeked his head out. His eyes instinctively looked at the wall across from the door. For a second he frowned, perplexed, then realized the girls were beside the door on the floor. "Oh, ladies. Very good." He looked down at the chart in his hand. "I need Jamila Phillips."

He opened the door another few inches and waited patiently while Mila unfolded herself from the floor.

The girls whispered "Good lucks" were cut off as the door shut behind her. The room was deathly quiet, like all of the noise had been sucked out of it.

"I'm Mr. George," the older gentleman said, extending his hand. He pumped Mila's hand lightly. "I'm the director of student services for the school system. Please place your bag in a corner and have a seat at the chair in front of the panelists' table when you're ready."

Mila quickly put on her jazz shoes and was in the chair within seconds. She crossed her feet to stop the tremors in her legs.

Mademoiselle Noelle, Mr. George, and Ms. Rexler sat behind a table.

"First, I need you to breathe," Mademoiselle said. She smiled broadly as Mila's breath came out in a swoosh. "Good. It's okay to be nervous. But we're just going to talk to you for a little bit. We have a few questions and then you'll do your jazz choreography for us. Okay?"

"Yes," Mila said, like a soldier accepting her orders.

Mademoiselle nodded to her fellow judges.

Ms. Rexler pushed a pair of specs higher onto her nose and looked down at the paper in front of her, then asked, in a rehearsed clip, "What does dance mean to you?"

Mila's legs jiggled as the question rolled around in her head. "Dance . . . ," she said, barely above a whisper.

Mademoiselle held up her hand. "It's okay to take time to think about your answer. But when you answer, speak up, please."

Mila sat up straighter. In the ballet audition, she'd been afraid looking at Mademoiselle would make her nervous. But her teacher's firm instruction comforted her. She nodded confidently and projected her voice.

"Since I was about five years old, my dad has made me and my brothers pick activities to do after school. And when we didn't pick one fast enough, he'd pick it for us."

Mr. George and Ms. Rexler chuckled softly under their breaths. Mademoiselle smiled knowingly.

"When the rec center put up posters about La May . . . I mean La Maison de Danse, it had a picture of this Black woman leaping. I had never seen anybody leap that high before," Mila said, relaxing at the memory. "She looked like she was flying and I knew I wanted to try it. It was the first time that I asked my dad about signing up before he could tell me to. And then when I walked into my first day of class, Mademoiselle Noelle was there and she was the one on the poster. It was like meeting a celebrity."

Mila's face turned hot. She felt silly admitting that, but the judges' curious faces prodded her on.

"That was only two years ago, but it feels like I've been dancing forever. Sometimes I don't even remember what I did every day before I started dancing. It's a big part of my life now. I . . ." She hesitated, not wanting to sound corny, like she believed TAG could change her life even though she really wanted it to. She cleared her throat and told the truth. "I feel like I need to dance because . . . it's where I feel safe."

She sat back in the chair and uncrossed her legs. There was nothing else to say.

Each judge scribbled something.

Mila felt her heart settling. She didn't know if what she'd said was enough. But it had been the truth.

CHAPTER
18

Tai sat up against the wall, eyes closed as the music behind the door played faintly. It sounded like something from a Broadway play—lots of trumpets and piano. Noelle sometimes gave them choreography to that kind of music and Tai didn't like it. It was dramatic and corny.

She was glad they had gotten to pick their own music for jazz. She was dancing to Big Daddy's "Get 'Em Girl." It was lots of bass and drums.

She drowned out the wacky music and went over her choreo. Her foot tapped to the rhythm as the beat filled her chest. Her lips mumbled the steps as she performed them in her head. She didn't hear the music. Didn't feel the air wash over her as the door opened beside her. Didn't notice the man standing above her until he said, "Me-tie Johnson?"

Tai's eyes popped open. It was the same guy who had been in the ballet auditions. She instinctively corrected him.

"It's Tay, Me-tay."

He glanced down at the paper, squinting, like maybe she was the one who had it wrong. He held the door open. "Sorry about that. This way, Ms. Johnson," he said, letting her march in ahead of him.

The nerves that had run away as she imagined her routine were back.

Two other judges sat at the table. One was a White woman with her hair in a tight dance bun. She held her head up, high and still. The other was a Black man with a head full of neat dreads. There was so much hair, Tai wondered what kept them back off his face.

He looked familiar. Or maybe it was that he at least looked like he probably knew something about dancing, real dancing not just ballet. Not like the snotty-looking woman or the nerdy-looking guy.

A chair sat in front of them. Tai assumed she was supposed to sit in it. No one instructed otherwise. She slid into the chair and sat her bag on her lap.

"I'm Mr. Hudson," the Black dude who walked her in said. "I'm president of the school board. To my left is Ms. Kirkland, director of the Romanov Ballet School and Mr. Sommers, founder of Hip-hop Heads."

Tai's face lit up. Hip-hop Heads was the only hip-hop dance studio around. She watched their videos all the time. She knew she'd recognized him.

As far as she was concerned, Mr. Sommers was her good luck charm. Having him in her interview had to be a sign. She doubted Ms. Romanov Ballet knew anything about jazz, and the other dude was just there from the school system so he definitely didn't know boo about jazz. But Mr. Sommers would. He'd see how good Tai was.

She sat up straight in the chair, praying they'd let her dance first.

Mr. Hudson dashed that hope immediately. "You can place your dance bag on the floor. We'll do the interview portion first."

Tai took her time putting the bag down, to get her face together. She hoped she didn't look as disappointed as she felt. She breathed loud into the floor, letting the scrape of her bag on the floor hide it, then sat back up. She plastered what felt like a smile on her face.

"Ready?" Mr. Hudson asked, throwing back his own smile. It looked fake.

Tai forced herself not to roll her eyes. "Yes," she said with more confidence than she felt.

Mr. Hudson sat back. That was Mr. Sommers's cue. His long dreads spilled over his shoulder and hung over the table as his eyes fixed on Tai. They were friendly eyes that didn't quite match with his gravelly voice.

"Miss Johnson, why do you want to be in the TAG program?"

Tai's mouth opened. Her lip hung in thought. It was the easiest question in the world. One she'd even expected, and still she didn't know how to answer.

"Take your time," Mr. Sommers said.

Why did she want to be in TAG?

Because Rollie was excited about it and sometimes the enthusiasm jumped off him and stuck to her. Because it would mean they'd share a bus ride from school to TAG classes. Because if she didn't make it, no way her and Bean would stay friends. She'd be left behind.

She knew she couldn't say that. Even if it was the truth.

Mr. Hudson's pen tapped softly on the table. Tai could see him fighting to look patient.

Ms. Romanov Ballet sat up even taller. Her eyes went slightly to the left, as if she was trying to signal Mr. Sommers to make Tai say something, before settling on the paper in front of her. It made Tai mad.

This was stupid. What did it matter why she wanted to get into TAG? Why couldn't they just let her dance?

Mr. Sommers's voice guided her back. "It's not a trick question, Metai." He imitated looking under his sleeve then shaking his head to show there was nothing there. It made Tai smile. He smiled back. "You could be honest with us and say that your mother or father or auntie is making you do it. We have about thirty more students to see and so probably a lot of the answers are going to sound the same. So honest answers are a nice break."

He flicked an eyebrow at his fellow judges. They chuckled, nodding.

"We're doing interviews because we want to hear from your mouth how you feel about your art or the program. Then when you dance for us, we get to see how you feel about it. Fair enough?" His gaze bore into Tai, pulling her head up and down in agreement. He folded his arms in front of him on the table. "So, why do you want to be in TAG?"

Tai spilled her guts.

"Because all of my friends are trying out. I think they think TAG is going to change their lives." She couldn't hold back a snort. "I don't think it will. I've been in other programs that were fun but didn't change anything. It seem sort of stupid to think TAG will."

Ms. Romanov Ballet's eyes widened. She wrote something down on Mr. Sommers's paper, not even hiding that she was talking about Tai right in front of her. Tai's throat clenched. She started to stop right there. Let them ask her what she wanted; it didn't matter. Then Mr. Sommers, without ever looking at the note, nodded for her to go on.

Tai kept her eyes on him as she talked. "I don't think TAG is going to change my life, but I don't want to be the only one not in it, either."

"Then is it fair to say it only matters to you if your friends make it?" Mr. Sommers asked calmly.

"I . . . I guess," Tai said, locked into answering honestly.

"That puts us in an odd position, doesn't it?" he asked.

Ms. Romanov Ballet forgot they were sitting behind an open table. She kicked Mr. Sommers lightly on the foot. "Jim, you're getting off course," she whispered.

"Maybe," Mr. Sommers said, never taking his eye off Tai. "But Metai had the courage to answer us honestly. I think it's only fair that we talk straight back."

As if knowing his place, Mr. Hudson remained silent. Ms. Romanov Ballet sighed and put her pen down.

Mr. Sommers looked down at the paper for a second, searching. "Look, Metai, there are one hundred students trying out for the dance program. That's more than any of the other disciplines. And we can only choose thirty. Do you understand that?"

Tai's head felt like it weighed a ton as she nodded.

"What I'm saying is, honesty aside, we could cut you just based on you not caring. It would actually make our jobs easier. But something tells me that there must be something else that's making you sit here besides peer pressure or not wanting to be left out." He crossed his legs. "One more chance to share."

"I'm good at jazz," Tai mumbled. His eyebrow went

up, a hook pulling the answer out of her. "And I love hip-hop. I'm a good dancer. But I'm not that great at ballet." She paused as Ms. Romanov Ballet glanced down at her paper as if looking for something. Tai couldn't read her expression. She didn't care what she thought anyway. She went on, talking to Mr. Sommers. "Sometimes it seems like you not a real dancer if you not good at ballet." The smug look on Romanov Ballet's face fueled her. "There gotta be other people trying out who not that great at ballet but good at other types of dancing. For real, if TAG is just for ballerina wannabes then it's not for me. And that's fine. But the packet said it was about all types of dance styles. And I'm down for that."

Finally there was silence.

If the other two were supposed to ask her questions, they'd either run out of time or didn't care to anymore. Mr. Sommers scribbled something as he said, "Thank you. Anytime you're ready, cue the music and show us how you feel about TAG."

Tai felt like she'd lost a ton. She could have floated up to the ceiling, she was so light. She was going to kill this audition. She felt it.

CHAPTER
19

The aroma of mozzarella and sausage met Mila at the door. Her mouth watered and her stomach rejoiced. Her dad had made lasagna. Her favorite and a special treat considering it was a Wednesday. Anything that took over thirty minutes to make was usually reserved for Sunday since the boys acted like they were starving as soon as they stepped off the school bus.

"What are we celebrating?" she asked, stepping through the door and startling Jeremy.

He raced into the kitchen. "Daddy, she's home."

Mila drew the smell of the bubbling pasta deeper

into her nose. She hadn't eaten much the last few days—audition anxiety and arguing with Tai had killed her appetite. Her stomach reminded her how good food could be.

A bouquet of balloons floated in the middle of the room. A small fish bowl sat in the middle of the coffee table full of water and pink flowers.

Her dad came out of the kitchen. His smile was a mile wide. Jeremy was behind him holding a big *You Rock* Mylar balloon. He shyly thrust it at her. "Here you go."

"Aww, thank you, Nut," Mila said. She rubbed his head.

Her dad wrapped her in a bear hug. "You're early. I knew I should have left work at noon." He pulled her toward the sofa. "We're making you a 'congratulations on surviving auditions' dinner. Tell us all about 'em."

Jeremy sat on the coffee table. His eyes ping-ponged between Mila and their dad. It filled Mila's heart. Being the only girl, still at home, made her the center of attention a lot, but not always in a good way.

JJ sauntered down the stairs. He leaned on the back of a chair. "So did you merc it or what?" he asked in greeting.

Mila collapsed onto the sofa. She folded her legs beneath her as she wondered where to start. The thought of being good enough to beat out a hundred other people sat on her confidence. "I mean, I think I did good," she said.

She replayed the day in her head. There had only been two other questions in the interview. The kind you could easily figure out what they probably wanted to hear. It had been the first time anyone had asked Mila why she wanted to be in TAG. She knew they were asking everybody the same thing, but the question had freed something inside of her. For the first time she shared her dreams of using dance to see the world outside of Del Rio Bay and it felt totally possible.

When it came time to dance, her nerves had finally calmed. They had a choice—make up their own or use a combination taught on day one of the auditions. She'd never been good at making up her own stuff and gladly used their choreo. Imagining herself in the La May dance room, she'd lost herself in the short routine. When it was over, Mademoiselle looked pleased. That was enough for Mila.

She shared as much with her family. Her dad's smile was so big Mila could count all his teeth.

"So quick, no thinking . . . you think you made it?" he asked.

It was one of his favorite tricks, making them answer on the spot without thinking. He said the first answer was usually the honest one.

"One minute yes and then the next minute no," Mila said with an apologetic shrug. It wasn't the kind of answer that usually went over well with her dad. His laugh reassured her.

He settled in, ready for every detail. "I think it's normal to feel that way. Did a lot of Black kids try out?"

Mila was happy to oblige every question he had. She was enjoying reliving it. But when JJ's eyes wandered to the kitchen, she let him off the hook by asking what she knew he was thinking. "How long before dinner is done, Daddy?"

JJ rewarded her with a grateful look.

"Another twenty minutes," her dad said.

"Can I go finish my game?" JJ asked.

"Your sister isn't done," her dad said, ready to get lecture-y. "Are you?"

"No, I am," Mila said. She stood up, giving JJ permission to roll out. "Plus I need to take a shower."

"Can I play?" Jeremy asked, following JJ. He pleaded

the entire way up the stairs, JJ growling no all the way.

"Jamila, wait," her dad said before she could get up the stairs. "I'm very proud of you."

She beamed back at him. "Thanks, Daddy."

"No, not just for doing well at the audition. You do good at whatever you put your mind to. That's just who you are." He walked over to her. His hand stroked her shoulder. "Once I said no to moving to the Woods, I wondered if maybe it could hurt your audition. I wasn't sure you even still wanted to try out." He cradled her head, turning it up to him. The gold flecks in his brown eyes twinkled at her. "You know, after we talked about it, I talked to Cinny." A ghost smile passed over his face. "She read me a little." He laughed. "Okay she put me on blast, as y'all kids say."

Cinny had never been afraid to speak her mind even to their dad. Mila wished she had the same courage.

"I have to admit, I was surprised you wanted to move with your aunt, but mostly I was hurt." He guided her so she was standing in front of him. He sat down on the bottom step. "When I let Cinny move, I knew I'd made the right decision and it was like a weight had lifted off me. Then once she was actually gone, that weight came back ten times heavier. It's not right to let somebody else raise your kids. And that's why I stepped it up because I didn't want to ever do that again. Then you come to me assuming I was going to let my only other baby girl go. And that thing shook me." He exhaled then gave her a fake smile. "Cinny said that I should let you move with them."

Mila's eyes lit up with hopeful curiosity. It instantly killed her dad's smile.

"And you still want to go even though you made it into TAG?" he said.

Mila frowned. "I don't know if I made it, Daddy."

His mouth twisted, half smile, half grimace. "What if I told you that you made it?"

Mila's mouth dropped open. Questions blazed across her mind. She'd made it? How would he know? When did he find out? Did everyone else make it, too?

Her dad's finger went to his lip, shushing her stunned silence. "I wasn't supposed to tell you. You look so shocked, baby girl. Did you really not think you were good enough to get in?"

"Daddy, some of these girls have been dancing forever. They were really good," she said, in open admiration.

"Yeah, but Jamila, this program was created for kids

like you." His eyes bored into her as if trying to pass a message without speaking it. Seeing her confusion, he held her hands and gently squeezed. "When Noelle proposed this program, she did it after seeing you dance. She wanted girls like you to have as many chances as possible."

The joy in Mila's heart fluttered uncertainly.

"Was I guaranteed a spot?" she asked.

"I didn't say all that." Her dad chuckled. "I'm saying, Noelle went into the audition looking for more Jamilas. Luckily the original Jamila did well and scored high."

Mila digested it, torn between relief and shock. She was a good dancer. A really good one. She wanted to twirl around the room in celebration.

Maybe getting into TAG would make living in the Cove better. Make living across from Mr. Bryant better. It made her want to tell her dad the truth about what had happened with Tai's father. Tell him how sick she'd been inside but assure him that now maybe everything would be okay. Her mind seesawed from anxiety to joy while her dad talked on.

"So how does it feel to be the poster child for a brand-new program?"

Mila gave into the joy dancing inside her. "Really

good. But I'm scared for my friends. Since TAG was made for kids 'like me,' does that mean we all made it?"

Her dad's hand went up like he was warding off a horde of reporters.

"That I don't know, baby girl. The auditions were real. Everybody may not make it." His eyes probed hers, doing his mind art thing. "So getting selected makes you feel good? You're not saying that for me, are you?"

"Dancing for the judges felt good," Mila said, letting herself fall back into the rush of the audition. She hugged her arms as they goose bumped with joy. "And Chrissy said being in TAG will be like being at a performing arts school. I think being around so many people really into dancing, singing, and all that would be like breathing new air."

He smacked his knee in triumph. "And that's what I hoped it would feel like." His huge smile returned.

"I think it'll be fun," Mila said. She sent up a silent prayer that they'd all made it.

"Good." He put his hands up to his mouth, like he was praying, too, before declaring, "Okay. You did something scary not knowing how it was going to turn out. It's only fair that I return the favor." His eyes closed as if he was consulting with himself, then they popped open. "If you still want to move in with Aunt Jacqi for high school next year, you can."

Mila gaped at her dad. "But I thought—"

He put his finger up, stopping her.

"I said no before and you still made lemonade out of lemons. That's something you and your brothers have to learn to do as long as we living here. But if you think living with Aunt Jacqi will make you happy, then I can support that." His eyes glistened. "I'mma hate losing another one of my baby girls. But—"

Mila threw herself into his arms. "You wouldn't be losing me, Daddy," she said, letting her own tears fall.

Her dad's grip was like a vise. She held on, not sure if she wanted to be let go.

CHAPTER
20

Tai reread the group chat.

Roll-O: *Aight so we all meeting at the rec in 15?*

Chriss-E: *Remember nobody look til we all there. Bet?*

She-da-Man: *Bet*

Jah-Mee-Lah: *Bet*

Yo'MChris: *Bet*

Mo'Betta: *Bet*

Somehow everyone thought it was the best thing since the Internet to meet at the rec center and find out together who had made TAG. Why would anybody want to be humiliated in public? It felt bad enough in private.

Like having your stomach punched into your throat.

She guessed she should have been grateful that Noelle had given her a heads-up. But it didn't change how much it hurt.

As the squad went back and forth on what time the list was going live, what time to meet, and ground rules on how to act when they saw the list, she thought about her own fate, already decided. Noelle had shown up at her house the night before.

Thank God Nona had been home. Her father had been a total jack butt when he answered the door, flirting with Noelle. Tai hadn't paid it much mind until she recognized the melody of Noelle's accent from the door. "Allo, Mr. Jown-sen. I'm Noelle, Metai's dance instructor. May I come in?"

He'd stood there staring her up and down like she was a pork chop he couldn't wait to chew.

Tai popped up beside him. "Hey, Ms. Noelle."

"How you doing? I'm Bryant," her father had said, putting his hand out. Instead of shaking Noelle's hand he'd kissed it. She'd laughed politely.

"Nona, Ms. Noelle is here," Tai called up the stairs. She watched her father make a fool of himself, insisting on making conversation.

"Umph, I wish all of Tai's teachers looked like you. So what, you French?"

"I'm from Montreal," Noelle said.

"Montreal?" His mouth corkscrewed as if she'd said *Mars.* "How you talking like that from Canada?"

"Excuse my son and forgive his manners. I swear I've raised him better," Nona said, bumping her son aside with her hip. "Have a seat, please."

Noelle sat in the overstuffed arm chair. She was bright and fresh in a sundress that left her toned shoulders bare. In their small living room, she looked like a flower growing in the middle of raggedy grass.

"I actually came to talk to Metai." She crossed her legs properly and looked from Nona to Bryant, unsure which of them to address, then settled on Nona. "Would it be okay if me and Metai talked . . . " Her lips pressed together in thought, for a single second, then her face cleared with knowledge. "In private. For just a minute?"

"Oh, of course," Nona said in her proper voice usually reserved for talking to White people. She got up and pulled at Bryant's shirt. He ogled Noelle, his glance going up her leg as he passed by.

Noelle got right to business. "Metai, I want to talk to you about TAG." She took Tai's wooden head nod for agreement. "You did not make it." She was up and by Tai on the sofa in a blaze. She held Tai by the shoulder, whispering as if they weren't alone. Her breath smelled like Doublemint gum. It blew in Tai's face as she talked furiously with the type of passion she used to teach when they were down to the last twenty minutes and everyone was tired. "Listen to me. You weren't rejected. You were placed on the wait list. And that is a good thing. Yes?" Her fierce stare forced Tai to agree. "Mr. Sommers was very impressed by you. He said you have raw talent. The type of talent that dance teachers love to get their hands on. We all want to be a part of molding a great dancer. What lowered your score was ballet technique." She waved it away. "You were not the lowest by any means. However, Mr. Sommers said that he is worried about your commitment to dance. Your score for the interview was . . . well, not good."

Tai immediately thought about the Romanov teacher and how her nose was turned up the whole interview. She'd probably given Tai a zero. Stinky wench.

And who were they anyway? None of them knew her.

Noelle's grip was relentless. She shook Tai's shoulders gently, forcing her to listen. "This lack of dedication, it is the problem I see in you as well. Metai, it is okay to care about something," she said, pleading. She nodded toward the window. "Out there, in the streets, yes, you must be a certain way. But in the studio and on stage you can be free. You can be who you want to be. But most of all you don't have to be ashamed to enjoy being free. Mr. Sommers and I both think that TAG would be good for you. But the scores were the scores. No?"

Tai hated when she did that *Yes* and *No* stuff. She was never sure how to answer. Not that Noelle gave her that chance.

"But there is good news. Maybe we have your grandma and poppa to come back now?"

Tai was reeling. Noelle seemed so nonchalant about the whole thing. You didn't make it and we need you to care more, but oh, now let's get your grandmother back out here.

Before she knew it, Noelle was back in the chair and Nona at her side. Her father hadn't bothered to come back downstairs. Likely Nona's doing.

Noelle was explaining the point system, sharing Tai's scores and explaining the wait list. Tai faded out. All she could think about was that she hadn't made it. Then it got quiet and she realized they had stopped talking.

"Would you like that, Tai?" Nona was asking, her eyebrows caterpillared. "I mean, you could take the bus to classes, I guess, and then I could pick you up after work."

"Classes?" Tai asked. Didn't Nona understand she hadn't made it into TAG?

"Mr. Sommers is offering you a scholarship to attend classes at Hip-hop Heads," Noelle said. She played mad. "I told him he has lots of nerves stealing my students. But he believes that you would fit in at his studio. I cannot disagree."

"I wouldn't be at La May anymore?" Tai asked, looking from Nona to Noelle. It was too much information to process. She listened through a haze.

"They're the hip-hop studio, right?" Nona asked.

"It is a full dance studio," Noelle corrected her. "But they specialize in hip-hop. Yes. And I believe Metai has an interest in that form. And sadly that is not my forte. I am what they call a bun head."

Noelle and Nona laughed.

"If you would still like to take classes at La Maison, you may," Noelle said. "But I believe that your schedule would be quite full. As I said, as number one on the wait list, if just one student does not accept the offer to enroll in TAG's dance program, you are next. H3. TAG. Together this is a lot. No?"

"Indeed it is," Nona said with an eye roll. "This girl's activities already take up what little money I make."

Noelle nodded in sympathy like she had a house full of kids to feed. She and Nona chatted, assuming Tai was mulling it over. Minutes later when Tai still hadn't answered, Noelle stood up and informed her she had some time to think it over but needed to decide soon. With a little more chitchat, she was gone.

To Nona it had been all good. "Looks like somebody answering your prayers after all that complaining you do about ballet class," she'd said.

Tai didn't have a comeback. Her hate for ballet wasn't a secret. But not getting into TAG hurt. Instead of admitting it to Nona, she'd only faked a smile and muttered, "I guess."

The next day she checked herself in the mirror. A black cropped T-shirt with the number one on the front. Black shorts and black Converse. All black like she was hitting up a funeral. It wasn't on purpose; the outfit had just come together like that.

The short side of her hair was getting bushy as it grew out. Weeks ago Nona had pointed out she needed a visit to the salon soon. First Tai had begged off thinking she might need it long for the stupid required dance bun. Not anymore. H3 dancers had all kind of hair styles.

She grabbed a water bottle and spritzed the hair, watching the poof turn into pretty curls.

She tied a white bandana around her head to finish off her gangster girl look. She could see herself wearing one of the H3 jackets with this outfit. She'd fit right in, too. She hoped.

If she was going to play down not making TAG, she had to believe it herself first.

She topped off the look with a pair of shades and raced down the stairs. When she opened the door, her father's voice called from the sofa. "Ay . . . Tai. Ay."

She pushed the screen door open, prepared to pretend she hadn't heard him when he shouted, "Ay . . . where your little friend Bean been at?"

"Why you asking?" Tai asked, her back to him. Her jaw was clenched tight as a fist.

"I haven't seen her since I ran those hardheads off. Just wondering what's up." He snickered. "She ain't go and get herself in trouble with one of them boys, did she?"

His sneaky little laugh echoed in her ear. Heh-heh. She hated that laugh. Her finger gripped the door. Heh-heh. She fought the memory bubbling its way into her mind—her, her father, and Bean in the backyard. That laugh. Heh-heh. It shimmered foggy in her mind, wavering into a real picture.

Nona had asked them to dig holes for a bunch of potted flowers. Tai hadn't wanted to but Bean thought it would be fun. And it had been, sort of, until her father came out there, standing on the back step talking on the phone, glancing over at them trying to give nonsense directions on how to plant a flower. He ended his call abruptly and walked over to them like he really had to play Head Gardener. He reeked of stale smoke. He planted himself between them, pointing to the ground, showing them where Nona usually put things.

The first time his hand brushed against Bean she moved down an inch, not much, just enough so his gestures wouldn't poke her. But then he moved, too. Tai saw it. And he pointed again. Then again. The fourth time, as his hand slid back, his fingers brushed, then lingered on Bean's breast.

Tai wished she hadn't seen it or the horrified look on Bean's face like she'd just seen someone rise from the dead. She wished she hadn't heard that stupid heh-heh laugh and him saying, "They're grapes now, but they gon' be solid oranges one day. Trust."

He'd walked off, leaving them both frozen.

In her head Tai ran into the house screaming for Nona, to tattle. If she'd done that, Nona would have handled it right then and there. He was high and probably drunk, too. She would have kicked him out and told him to stay away until he got himself cleaned up. He would have listened that time because Nona would have been more furious than she'd ever been. And then he would have come back clean and been a real father. One who worked a real job and helped her with homework and came to her dance recital. If she'd run into the house. But she hadn't.

Instead, she'd stared after his back, afraid to look Bean in the eyes. When she finally turned around, she played it off like it was normal for a grown man to do that. "He's so ignorant. Just ignore him. I know I do."

She prayed so hard in her head that Bean would go along, her temples pounded.

Bean was frozen beside her, staring down at the

ragged holes they'd dug for the flowers. A few minutes later she mumbled something about having to get home and shot out of the yard like lightning.

The first couple of days, Tai had wanted to apologize a hundred times, but they'd never talked about it again. She knew her father had gone too far. But Tai hadn't known what to do. If Bean had said something, anything, maybe it would have been different. They could have told Nona together. When Bean didn't bring it up, Tai really thought she'd forgotten about it. It was just another one of those messed-up things that happened, sometimes, in the Cove.

They'd seen other wack stuff in the hood. Afterward people kept it moving. Like the time they were taking the shortcut to the Wa and saw Lil Mario lying in the middle of the path. Tai thought he was dead for sure. He had gotten into somebody's stash. They had gotten help just in time. It took days for Tai to forget how he'd looked, face ashy and his chest still like he wasn't breathing. They'd talked about it for days. The whole hood was out to celebrate when he got out the hospital. He was fine and like usual, life went on.

But life hadn't gone on like normal, and Tai hadn't realized why until it was too late. She kept saying Bean was different, because Bean was and had been since that day. Her not telling Tai she'd talked to Rollie wasn't like Bean at all, but deep down Tai knew it wasn't 'cause Bean was scheming. She was just . . . different.

Standing there watching her father lay on the couch, not a care in the world, Tai realized now how much that day had changed Bean.

Fury burned in her gut until it scorched her throat. She was at the edge of the sofa in three steps, chest heaving, eyes bugging.

"Girl, what's wrong with you?" her father asked, putting bass into his voice.

She stared him down. "Why you asking about Bean?"

"I just told you why." He scowled. "You needa watch yourself. You getting too grown, Metai. I'mma tell Momma."

"You don't never have spit to say to me unless you asking about Nona. Ever. You probably would never even talk to me, for real, if you wasn't too lazy to find out stuff for yourself." A single tear fell and dangled on her chin. She swiped at it angrily, scratching herself. "You don't ask me 'bout school. Dance. Who my friends are. But out the blue you gon' ask about Bean?"

He laid back down, his body taking up the whole length of the sofa, and stabbed the remote at the TV. Tai walked in front of it before he could click up the sound.

"Stop playing, Tai," he threatened.

"Don't ask me about Bean no more," she said, almost polite in her anger.

He sat up straight. Newly alert. They'd battled back and forth before, but never like this. He put strength in his voice to back her down. "Don't tell me what to do. Remember, I'm your father."

"Youn ever act like one," Tai spat. She stepped closer until she was only inches from her father's angry and confused face. Her words were a whisper. "Don't ask me about Bean no more or I'm telling Nona what you did."

Bryant Johnson's eyes narrowed as he recoiled from her. "I know that's not a threat."

Her father had never dared hit her. But the certainty that he never would was gone. His eyes flickered up and right as he searched his memory for what she was talking about.

"What lie you gon' tell her this time?" he sneered.

Tai didn't want to say the words out loud. It would make it too true. But she made them come out. "About the time you touched Bean." A stomach pain made her wince.

Her father's rant filled the entire house. "Man, you crazy. Momma let you get away with mess but she ain't gonna believe something like that. And you lying anyway."

Tai's head shook vigorously. "No, I'm not. Just 'cause you was too high to remember don't mean I'm lying."

Uncertainty shadowed his face. The number of times he'd come to the house drunk or high doing and saying stupid stuff were too many to count. Most times Nona either sent him away or off to his room to sleep it off. He hardly ever remembered the next day. He'd gotten used to getting the cold shoulder for a few days and was an expert at apologizing and promising to never do whatever he'd done again.

Nona always forgave. Tai never did.

"If I tell Nona, she probably kick you out for good," Tai warned. She stepped back as he stood up.

"Don't be saying no stuff like that, Metai." His finger wagged in her face. "Playing your little games with Momma to stay on her good side one thing. But don't be telling lies like this."

Tai was unflinching. "It's not a lie." She waited on him to smack her and make good on the threat he made every time they got into it. If that was what it cost, she would take it. It would force her to tell Nona everything and explain what would make him mad enough to hit her. She wished on it, daring him with her eyes. She owed it to Bean. "It's not a lie," she croaked again. When she realized he wasn't going to strike, she shot the last bullet. "If you think I'm lying, tell on me. Tell Nona I'm lying."

His eyes sliced her but he sat back down on the sofa, jaw and hands clenched.

The air went out of Tai. She walked away on spaghetti legs and sat on the front stoop, shaking.

CHAPTER
21

The crew was spread out. They sat on the wall outside the rec center, giddy with anxiety.

Roland and Chris were freestyling. One would spit a verse, then the other. They had rhymes for days. It was like if they stopped they'd have to talk about it some more. Who was in? Who was out? They hadn't talked about anything else the last two days. Group chats. Side chats. Text messages. The torture was in the silence. Especially for Mila.

She hated that she already knew. She'd almost told Chrissy because it had been painful to watch her new friend's confidence dwindle to nothing. Mila sat by silently as she obsessed over every step she'd taken, every answer she'd given or hadn't given wanting to assure her, "If I made it, you had to make it." But she'd been too afraid to trust Chrissy with the secret. Secrets had a way of backfiring.

Simp stationed himself next to Roland, like he could feel him slipping away. He had one leg up on the wall and a basketball cradled under his arm. He boosted Roland on, the hype man, shouting, "Yeah, son," "That's hot, B," every few bars.

Mila sat between Mo and Chrissy. Her long legs stretched out like two pieces of dark licorice in her homemade jean shorts. The night before, while on the phone with Chrissy, she had decorated them with squiggles and shapes in puffy paint. Chrissy had on a similar pair covered in puffy polka dots. Their over-the-phone craft session had been successful.

Sheeda stood in front of them telling the story of a girl who auditioned as a lost ball wandering the street trying to get back home to its owner. She twirled in a circle, looked around, lost, then spun again. It was cracking them up. Sheeda was making fun of the girl, but she was good.

Mila hoped she'd made it. She hoped everyone had.

She watched as Tai came up the street, in no hurry to reach them.

Her heart fluttered. Whenever she saw Tai, it felt like another showdown was waiting in the wings to pop off. Still, watching her walk up alone ate at Mila. Tai could be too much, but she wasn't all bad. Mila knew that better than anyone.

No one else knew Tai was afraid of heights. She wouldn't even go on the monkey bars.

No one else knew how at the end of sad movies she cried while yelling at the screen, "Why make sad movies? That's so stupid."

No one but Mila.

Figuring Tai would move Simp aside and go sit by Roland, she put her attention back on Sheeda and her story.

"Did y'all look at the list without me?" Tai asked, plunking down beside her.

Mila went along with the fragile peace, praying it wasn't a trap. "They haven't posted it yet."

Roland spit his last rhyme. He put his hand out and Chris gripped it, then pounded him on the back. "Your verses are beast, son."

"Yours, too," Chris said. "Shoot, maybe you should

have auditioned for vocal art."

Roland grinned. "Ay, I could be that double threat."
He looked down the line at Tai. "What took you so long?"

"I had to clean my bathroom before I left. I
don't need hear Nona's mouth," Tai said. There was
grumbling assent. Who hadn't been held up having to
do a last-minute chore or listen to a final instruction?

Noelle came around the corner. Her short pixie was
curly. She had on a white net shirt that hung off one
shoulder and a pair of navy blue linen shorts. She looked
odd without dance clothes on. A large piece of yellow
construction paper was limp in her hand. She shook it,
trying to keep it upright. Spying the group, she walked
right over. "I trust everyone's here waiting for this?" She
rattled the paper at them. "I love the enthusiasm."

"Oh my God, I'm not ready," Sheeda squealed. She
put her hand over her chest.

"I am," Mo said.

"Good luck to everyone," Noelle said, looking each
of them in the eye.

Mila picked at a loose piece of paint on her shorts. If
she looked at Mademoiselle, everyone would know she
already knew. She didn't breathe again until her dance
teacher stepped out of the circle and taped the paper to

the rec center door. Once Noelle disappeared inside the rec, Chris was the first one up. "Come on, let's do this."

The group walked in a cluster. They stopped dead center of the door. Simp lagged behind. He dribbled the ball, slow, letting long seconds build before he let it hit the ground again. The pinging of the ball was jarring. But its rhythm helped Mila focus.

They all stared at the six pieces of white paper glued to the yellow board. The names went on and on.

"Man, how do you read the list?" Roland shouted, confused.

Mo figured it out first. "It's in alphabetical order but all the disciplines are separate." She stepped forward and ran her finger down the first list. "This one is for drama."

Sheeda slapped her hands across her eyes. "I can't look."

Mo's finger slid, then stopped.

"Is that my name?" Sheeda asked, peeking.

Mo blew out a breath. "You were wait-listed, Sheeda."

Sheeda peered up at the list. "What does that mean?"

"It means if somebody else who made it decides not to do it, then you're in," Chrissy said, patting Sheeda's shoulder.

"So I can still maybe make it?" Sheeda asked. Her eyes searched around the cluster.

"What number on the list is she?" Chris asked.

Mo, happy in the role as announcer, checked. "It has a number three next to it."

"So you need somebody to drop out and then wait list people one and two have to not want to do it, either," Chris explained. "Or three people have to drop it. Either way, for real, it can happen."

"I mean that's better than not making it at all, right?" Sheeda asked.

There was chorus of "Yeah" and "True."

Mo was already back on the list. "The music list is next," she said, without turning around. Her finger scanned a small list, then dropped down to a longer list. "Oh my God. Okay. Rollie and Chris, both of y'all in."

They gave each other a pound. Roland's entire face was a smile.

"Ay, yo, I meet y'all on the court," Simp said. He walked away, slamming the ball into the ground.

"Yo, we catch up in a minute," Roland called out.

Simp gave him a thumbs-up without looking back.

"Is he okay?" Chrissy asked.

Roland watched him go. He seemed like he was

wondering the same thing himself, then he affirmed, "Yeah, he good." Him and Chris gripped hands once more, congratulating each other.

Sheeda shushed them. "Come on, Mo. Get to dance."

"I'm trying to," Mo said. Her neck strained, trying to read every list fast. Her eyes skimmed all the way down then went back up. She slowed herself down and started over.

"Well?" Tai asked.

Mila couldn't help it. She snaked her arm around Tai's and held on. It felt like the world was going to collapse, no matter the outcome. She wanted to run but her feet were cemented into the sidewalk. She hissed in utter relief when Tai's arm held on.

"I feel sick," Mila whispered.

"Me, too," Tai whispered back. Suddenly she shouted, "Mo, wait."

Mo scowled. "But I found—"

"I didn't make it," Tai blurted.

"Aw man, that's messed up," Roland muttered.

The crew clustered around Tai.

Tai's arm trembled. Mila squeezed gently and it calmed.

"I guess Noelle thought I'd flip or something if she

didn't tell me first," Tai said with a humorless laugh. "So she let me know I didn't make it. I'm on the wait list, too."

"Did she say where on the wait list?" Chris asked, glancing over his shoulder at the list.

Tai put up a finger.

"One is good," Sheeda said. "Right, Chris?"

"One is real good," he agreed. "People always trying out and then dropping out of these programs. If you one, I think you definitely in. Watch."

"Why would they audition if they not gonna actually do it?" Mo asked.

"Look y'all, don't be feeling sorry for me or try and boost me up," Tai said gruffly, then added in a softer voice, "No shade. But I've known since last night. I'm not cool with it, but I'm not tripping, either."

"Would you accept it if somebody dropped?" Chrissy asked, peering at her.

Tai's mouth pursed in thought.

"Man, yeah, she'd take it," Roland said.

Mo laughed. "Well, of course she gon' say yes now."

Tai swiped at her. "Dang, Mo. Don't be letting out my game."

"Would you, though?" Sheeda asked. "I mean, I know I would."

"I would," Tai admitted, with a little head shrug.

"Cool. People have until the second of September to drop. You good," Roland said, all confidence. "Go 'head, Mo. Finish up. I know Chrissy ready kirk not knowing."

Chrissy's laugh was high and nervous. "I am, sort of."

"I already saw." Mo grinned. "Me, Chrissy, and Bean got in." She touched Tai's shoulder, eyes sad. "Sorry, Tai. I was still looking for your name when you told me to stop. I sort of had already figured you hadn't made it 'cause I went through the J's twice."

"It's good," Tai said quietly.

"This gonna be crazy, y'all. I'm telling you," Roland said. He fiddled with his hat, crushing the lid gently. "Like we ready to be on some performing arts stuff when school start."

"Can y'all send up a prayer for me and Tai, though . . . that we make it?" Sheeda asked. "I mean for-real prayers. Not just saying you will."

Mila rubbed her back. "We will."

"Let's head to the court for a while," Roland suggested.

The herd began to move. Mila stayed rooted.

"What's wrong?" Tai asked, stopping.

It took a few seconds before their friends realized they'd stopped. "What y'all doing?" Mo yelled back at them.

"Tai can have my spot," Mila said. She hadn't intended to say it in front of the group, but it was out.

"I don't want your spot, Bean," Tai said. "I told you I'm fine. Look, if I make it into TAG, cool, but what I didn't say was that H3 want me to come dance with them."

Mila's eyes widened. "Tai, they do? That's so good."

Tai smiled shyly. It looked funny on her, but Mila couldn't help smiling with her. She wasn't sure what to do with the new information. H3 was perfect for Tai. It was better than TAG, really.

The crew edged closer but stopped short of rejoining the girls, like they knew whatever was happening was between her and Tai. Mila pushed her shades to the top of her head. She turned her face away from the sun and looked Tai dead-on.

"My dad said I could go to the Woods if I want. I mean for high school." It hurt her face to keep smiling, but she glued it on as Tai's mouth popped open into a tiny O. "All you need to get into TAG is for one person to drop out. So maybe that's how it should be anyway. You take my spot."

Mo was beside them in seconds. "Mila, no. Like Chris said, other people probably drop out. Y'all can both be in it." She looked from Tai to Mila, apologizing with her eyes to one and pleading with the other. "Just wait till the second and see."

No one else joined Mo's campaign.

Tai crossed her arms. "I'll be all right." There was a crack in her voice then it was gone, replaced with the bossiness Mila knew well. "You'd be crazy not to do TAG. That's all you. Just do it."

Mila looked over Mo's head at the curious crew. "Can y'all give me and Tai a minute, please? We'll catch up." Mo started to object. Mila shook her head at her. "We be right behind y'all, Mo."

Mila waited until they were around the corner and out of sight. She sat on the ledge. Tai leaned against the wall, shoulders sagging. Before Mila could say anything, Tai took off her sunglasses and clipped them onto her T-shirt. Her eyes were red rimmed.

"You said you were okay with not getting into TAG, but it look like you've been crying," Mila said.

Tai's nod was slow and heavy. "It wasn't about TAG, though."

Mila leaned in. "What's wrong?"

"I don't have a best friend anymore," Tai said, then burst into tears.

Voices carried from the court. Otherwise the area around the rec was quiet.

Mila wished she hadn't sent the crew away. Then again, she knew Tai would have never cried in front of anyone. Whether they were beefing or not, there were still some things that were just between them. She touched Tai on the shoulder. As complicated as things always seemed, they were friends. And had been forever.

Mila's heart flooded with emotion as the memories they shared rushed over her. "Tai, we're still friends."

"Not like we used to be," Tai said, chest hitching as the tears dried up.

Mila couldn't deny that. She went back to safer ground. "You're my girl, though, that's why I want you to take my spot in TAG."

"If you want to move to the Woods, just say so. Don't—" Tai stopped, took a breath. Her eyes fixed on Mila's. "I understand why you want to move. And I'm not mad. Not anymore."

Mila looked past Tai at the huge yellow poster on the rec door. "Why do you think I want to move?"

Tai sniffed. "Because I don't know how to be a good friend. Not like Chrissy."

"I never said that," Mila said, defensively.

"You don't need to," Tai snapped.

Mila shrank from the familiar anger between them. She was ready to say *Take the spot and have a nice life* until Tai switched gears. "I been acting real grimy lately. I'm sorry."

Braids wriggled around Mila's face as she shook her head. "No. If I had just told you I ran into Roland, it wouldn't seem like I was hiding it." Her eyes closed as she confessed. "But I was hiding it."

"Why?" Tai asked, eyes wide.

"Because it's like we can only be friends if I do what you want or say what you want me to say." Mila couldn't stop anger from edging into her voice. "I can never just be me without it being lame or stupid or crazy. And you dog me in front of everybody like you can't wait to make fun of something I did or said."

Tai slumped against the wall. "I just be playing," she said.

Mila wanted to back off, but the words kept flowing. "Yeah, but it hurts my feelings. And I know if I had told you I saw Roland, you would have gotten mad that I saw him. Even though I didn't have nothing to do with him being in the Woods, you would have made it my fault somehow." She looked off past Tai, unable to meet her gaze. "Then sometimes it feels like you blame me for what happened that day in the backyard. Do you think I wanted him to do it? Is that why you've been so mad?"

"Bean, no," Tai exclaimed. She wiped at fat tears dropping, but replacements arrived immediately. Her head hung. Her voice was just above a whisper. "It's not you I'm mad at. I was never mad at you. It's him. And I should have said something when it happened. I'm sorry."

"I don't want to fight anymore," Mila said.

"Me, either," Tai said eagerly. There was a pause, then, "If you want, we can tell Nona what my father did, together."

The words sent a shock through Mila. She barely felt Tai's fingers wrap around hers.

"I think we should tell," Tai said.

"I . . . I don't want to," Mila said. She wiggled her fingers out of Tai's. "My dad will flip. I don't want him getting in trouble for trying to fight yours. Don't. We shouldn't. Just . . . just take my spot in TAG. Then next year I'll move with my aunt and—"

The words broke off. She hung her head and began to sob.

Tai was up on the ledge, her arms around her in an instant. She peeked under Mila's curtain of braids. "If you want to move, I'm for-real cool with that. But don't go 'cause of my stupid father." She swatted at a braid tickling Mila's cheek. "I think we have to tell."

Mila stared out into the neighborhood. Her dad saw a different Cove than she did. Everything he did was to make it a nicer place to live. She couldn't imagine what would happen if she told him about Mr. Bryant. What people would say. What her dad might do. How it would change things. Would it make them better or worse?

"We'll do it together," Tai said, this time stronger than before.

Mila closed her eyes. Her temples throbbed.

Tai's voice came from far away, almost a chant. "Together. We'll tell Nona together."

CHAPTER
22

For 106 days, 12 hours, and 10 minutes, Jamila Phillips had kept a secret. She was convinced that if Tai took her spot at TAG, she could keep the secret forever.

I don't want to tell, she texted Tai.

That was that.

Her dad came in just as Tai's message buzzed back. To Mila the vibration sounded angry. She tucked the phone under her leg, without looking at the message, and forced herself to be normal.

Her dad ducked his head and sat on her bottom bunk. He looked around the room like he was seeing it for the first time. The springs of her mattress squeaked under his weight. He bounced on it lightly, patting it.

"If you go to Aunt Jacqs I might let Jeremy have your mattress. He needs a new one." He poked gently at her side. "That's my not-so-sneaky way of asking have you made a decision?"

He hadn't been the only one waiting on it. Her friends had been begging her to stay. Chrissy had worked on her the most, killing her with, "You're the realest friend I have here. Please stay."

For one millisecond Mila had been tempted. She really liked Chrissy and didn't want to leave her hanging. But she couldn't stay. Still, she tried putting off.

"I still have a few more days to decide," she said, with forced cheer.

Her dad's eyebrow shot up. "I didn't think it would be that hard a decision." He couldn't hide his smile. "So you don't want to move to the Woods?"

His eagerness broke Mila's heart. She wished she wanted to stay for the same reasons he wanted her to stay. Love of their neighborhood. Excitement for TAG. "I want to but I . . ." She wracked her brain for a good lie and came up totally empty. "I mean, I don't want to . . . but I'm scared not to."

Her dad went rigid beside her. "What's going on, Jamila?" He cupped her knee in his hand, squeezing firmly. "You know you can tell me anything."

She buried her face in his chest.

"What is it, baby girl? Did somebody threaten you? What?"

His heartbeat was loud in her ears. His voice louder. She kept herself glued to him, afraid to meet his eyes.

"Mr. Bryant . . . touched me."

She said it so low she wasn't sure he'd heard her at first. But the sudden gallop of his heart made her lift her head in alarm.

The look on his face frightened her more. His eyes were big and wild. His mouth opened and closed. No words came out for what seemed like minutes until he finally asked, "Touched you where? When was this?"

"He—he . . ." She talked down to her lap. "He touched my breast." Fearing the worst in his silence, she looked up and added quickly, "Just once."

He shot up, nearly whacking his head on the top bunk.

"It doesn't matter if it was just once, Jamila." He paced the small room, covering the distance from the bed to the door in only two long strides. "Tell me everything."

He pulled her desk chair up to the bed. She relayed the story, apologizing over and over, scared of the anger she felt popping off him like electricity.

His hand squeezed her shoulder. "It's not your fault, baby girl." His words were gentle, but seemed to barely slip out between his clenched teeth. "I need to handle this," he said at the door in what seemed like a single step.

"I want to go to Aunt Jacqi's because I don't want you to fight Mr. Bryant, Daddy," she blubbered. "Just let it go. If I leave, then he can't ever do it again." She ran up and hugged him from behind. "Can't we just let it go? I won't go to Tai's anymore." She fell over herself to promise anything to keep her dad from going across the street. "Or you can send me to Aunt Jacqs' this school year. I . . . . I just don't want you to get in trouble."

He loosened her grip enough so he could turn around.

Mila immediately hugged him tighter as if it would root him there forever. "Don't go over there, Daddy. Please," she cried. "Please."

CHAPTER
23

*Boom*BoomBoomBoomBoom.

Tai heard the pounding on the door the same time Bean's text came through: *my dad knows!*

The spit in her mouth dried up. This was going to be bad. Like, no-way-everybody-in-the-hood-won't-know-what's-happening bad. She jumped off her bed and stood, unsure whether to go downstairs or hide.

"Who in the world is knocking on the door like that?" Nona yelled. Her shoes clicked across the hallway's hardwood and tip-tapped down the stairs as she raced to the door, ready to confront whoever had the nerve to knock on her door that hard.

BOOM . . . BOOM.

The door sounded like it was ready to bust open.

Tai put her face in her hands, breathed in, held it until her lungs burned, then let the hot air go into her hands. She prayed to herself to get her heart out of her throat and back where it belonged, then tiptoed to the top of the stairs. She sat in the dim stairwell, hugging her knees. There was no need to creep down any farther; she could hear fine. The whole neighborhood could, probably.

"Jamal, what is wrong with you? Knocking on my door like that," Nona said, voice raised for combat.

"Is Bryant home, Sophia?" Mr. Jamal asked.

Tai hugged herself tighter. Her father was in his usual spot on the sofa, willing to let Nona handle whatever the commotion was.

"What's the problem?" Nona asked.

She'd already calmed down. Mr. Jamal wasn't the first person to come to their door for something her father did. Owing people money, warrants for failure to appear in court on stupid things like speeding tickets and suspended driver's license.

And no surprise, she hadn't heard a peep out of her

father. He let Nona fight his battles all the time. Tai's jaw clenched. She closed her eyes tight and focused on the loud voices.

"Look, I don't mean no disrespect to you or your house, Sophia. But I need talk to Bryant. Not through you, either."

"Well, you coming about it wrong, knocking on my door like you the police or something," Nona said as if talking to a child. "Come in. The whole world don't need to know our business." The door squeaked closed. Nona's steps clacked then fell silent as she crossed into the living room. "Bryant, get up. I know you hear Jamal asking for you. What in the world is going on?"

Unbelievably her father's voice was sleepy. He'd for real slept through Mr. Jamal's pounding. Tai couldn't hear what he mumbled, only Nona's testy "Boy, I don't know what he wants. But he near knocked the door down. Get up."

Mr. Jamal must have been standing by the door because Tai hadn't heard his footsteps.

Her body was tense. Nona was probably between them now, standing by the couch. What if Mr. Jamal came at her father? He was usually the peacemaker. She couldn't see him fighting anybody, but if he ever would, this would be the time.

Tai slipped down on her butt, one step at a time until she was as close as she could get before her shins appeared in the space between the top and bottom of the staircase, then dared one last step so she could see through the space into the living room.

"What's up, man?" her father asked, his voice thick with sleep. He wiped at his eyes.

Mr. Jamal's voice was scary calm. "I'mma need you to get yourself together, Bryant. I'm not gon' sit here and try talk to you while you half out of it." He straightened up to his full height, arms folded. It made him look like a security guard. It also made him look like he was blocking the door in case her father decided to run. "I can wait."

"Jamal, what is going on?" Nona asked. There was real worry in her voice now.

Tai's father blew out breath, then stood up. He swiped his hands across his eyes, then folded his own arms. "What's up, Jamal? Me and you ain't never had no beef."

"This ain't about no beef, Bryant. We not sixteen." Mr. Jamal took one step forward, then seemed to stop himself. His arms stayed folded, tight. Tai could see the muscle in his arm bulge. "Jamila just told me something that . . . " His lips pursed. He seemed to breathe through his nose before opening them again. "You know what, man? You always been a screw-up. But . . . "

"Jamal," Nona snapped. "Don't sit here in my house coming at my son like that. He a man just like you. Say what you came to say."

The look on Mr. Jamal's face made Tai want to run down and pull Nona out of the way. But whatever thoughts he had, he kept them in check. "Jamila said you touched her breast." He spat the last word, like he couldn't wait to get it out of his mouth.

Nona gasped.

Tai's heart pounded into her knees. She hadn't realized she was curled into a ball. She exhaled quietly as possible between her knees.

"Jamal that kind of accusation—" Nona said, then stopped. She peered at Tai's father. Then back at Jamal. "Bryant . . ." She grabbed the back of the sofa like she needed it to balance. "I . . . Bean wouldn't make up something like this, but—"

"There is no *but*, Sophia," Mr. Jamal said. "I know my children better than anybody. They don't lie. So no sense in us questioning if Jamila telling the truth. I don't have time for that."

Nona nodded softly.

"Man, look, I don't know what games Bean and Tai playing, but I ain't never touch nobody," her father said with a defiant snort.

Nona frowned. "What does Tai have to do with this?"

Tai crouched lower as Nona's head swung in the direction of the stairs.

"Bean said it happened in April," Mr. Jamal said.

"April?" Nona's hand pressed her chest. "Is that why she went away this summer? Jamal I . . . I'm sorry."

"Momma, I ain't touch nobody," her father whined. "She saying this for attention or something."

"Don't nobody keep a secret like that if they want attention, Bryant," Nona said. Her voice sounded tired. "Jamal . . . are you sure? I mean is Bean sure that it wasn't some kind of . . . mistake? Did she maybe misinterpret—"

Mr. Jamal's head shook firmly once to the left, once to the right. His arm muscle popped. It seemed like if he let go, all hell would break loose. Tai silently prayed he'd never unfold his arms.

"The details were clear. She's not making it up," Mr. Jamal said.

Nona's head slowly nodded. Her eyes never left Mr. Jamal's. She believed.

Mr. Jamal exhaled hard. "Bean's word is enough. I'm not here to compare stories." He took another step forward.

Tai calculated he could be at her father's throat in only two more long steps. Her father must have done the same math, because he took a step back.

"Stay away from my daughter, Bryant. I don't think I should have to tell you that, but since your mother here to hear it, I'm saying it out loud." Mr. Jamal's eyes were locked into her father's. "That way if you play dumb or forget that I said it and decide to go near Bean, there's a witness to say I warned you."

Her father's hands jammed into the pockets of his skinny jeans. Only the first few fingers fit. His arms winged out. It made him look like he was about to do the chicken dance. He challenged Mr. Jamal. "Then you tell your daughter don't be over here hanging with Tai and a bunch of hardheads."

The glint of joy in his eyes, like he really had something over her and Bean, made Tai want to scream. Mr. Jamal didn't miss a beat. "Don't worry. As long as you live here, Bean won't ever be over."

Tai's heart broke immediately at the finality in Mr. Jamal's word. Her back hitched silently as she unsuccessfully gulped the tears back.

"Man, look. Believe what you want. I didn't do nothing," her father said with a shrug.

"How do you know, Bryant?" Nona asked quietly. "If Jamal told me the exact date it happened. Where it happened. How it happened . . . could you give me the same amount of information to prove you didn't do it?"

Nona's directness threw him off for a second, but he stayed the course, confident he was the victim. "Probably not. But I ain't no child molester. So why would I touch her?"

"Why would she lie?" Nona pressed.

"Attention," he said. "Why would I lie?"

Nona and Mr. Jamal answered at the same time. "Because you a drug addict."

The words pushed her father back a step. He looked from one to the other, trying to get himself together. Nona beat him to words. "You barely know where you live when you get high. How you gonna sit here and tell me you know for sure you didn't fondle that little girl?"

"Fondle?" Her father's mouth screwed up. "Momma, get outta here with that. You know I'm not like that."

Nona blew a breath toward the ceiling. She walked over to Mr. Jamal.

"I'm sorry. I'm really sorry."

"Momma? Momma?" her father called out, his voice high-pitched. "You gon' sit here and believe this? You know that ain't me. I'm not like that."

Nona talked on. "I don't even know what to say. If there's anything I can do . . ." She covered her eyes. Her shoulders shook hard as she wept. Mr. Jamal went to put his arm around her and Nona pressed her hand on his chest, gently pushing him. "No. Bean is the one hurt. I'm just . . . I'm just tired. I'm sorry, Jamal. Whatever you need, you let me know."

For the first time Mr. Jamal's eyes softened. "It's not your fault, Sophia."

Nona's chuckle was bitter. "It's not, but it's my burden."

Tai hated the sympathy she saw in Mr. Jamal's eyes. It was confirmation that her family was really messed up. Like she needed any more proof, her father ranted on, muttering under his breath like somebody crazy, defending himself, peppering every other sentence with "Get outta here, man" and "That ain't me. I ain't the one."

Mr. Jamal patted Nona's shoulder. He looked over at Tai's father and opened his mouth to say something, then didn't. The second he walked out the door, her father began pleading his case, begging Nona to "think about it," asking her why would he do something like that.

It fell on deaf ears. Nona walked out of his face. As her footsteps tapped heavily, slowly toward the stairway, Tai scampered up the stairs and dove onto her bed. She knew Nona probably heard her skittering feet and hands smacking the wood as she raced. She couldn't pretend she was asleep or hadn't heard. So she sat cross-legged on the bed and waited.

When Nona's face appeared in the doorway, they just looked at each other. She didn't ask, but Tai felt the question in the air. Saw it in the tears leaking down her grandmother's face. She nodded once in answer.

Nona covered her mouth, choking back sound. She shook her head and nearly ran down the hall to her room.

Tai stared at the empty doorway. Lost.

EPILOGUE—
MILA'S NOVEMBER

Mila stood on her front stoop, waiting patiently for Tai so they could walk to the bus stop. A chill ran down her back as wind swirled around her bare legs. Fall had elbowed summer out of the way quickly. She stubbornly held on by wearing a dress that should have been put away three weeks earlier.

The wind nudged again. She sank deeper into her new jacket. It was black nylon with a dancer in full leap embroidered across the back over the words *La Maison de Danse*. The jacket and dress didn't match. But she wouldn't be alone. She couldn't think of one person in TAG that didn't wear something to rep their discipline. They were almost worse than the football players and cheerleaders who always stayed geared up.

Her head craned up the street, then down, waiting for Chrissy, Mo, and Sheeda to appear on the horizon. Somehow she avoided staring directly across at Tai's house.

Mr. Bryant didn't stay there anymore. She didn't know where he lived now. She didn't want to know. Still, she was always afraid his face would be grinning back at her the very day she decided to let her gaze rest on the front door.

She'd gotten better, every day, at acting like Tai's house was invisible. She couldn't remember the last time she'd even walked on that side of the street. Thankfully, Tai seemed to understand that was the price of Mila staying in the Cove because she never asked Mila about coming over. Not once, since it had all gone down.

The night her dad had confronted Mr. Bryant was bad. But it wasn't the worst.

No amount of begging had stopped her dad from filing charges. Within days, everyone knew. Not just everyone in the Cove, but the world. At least it felt like the world to Mila.

JJ had been ready to fight Mr. Bryant. Their dad had squashed that real quick with a stern look and a firm "We don't handle things that way in this house, Jamal Jr."

Mila had heard their whispered voices again, later. JJ sounded like he was crying. Whatever their dad had said calmed it. And for a while JJ was nicer to Mila.

She had been glad when their usual bickering started back up. As annoying as arguing was, having JJ be super-nice wracked her nerves more.

Then there were her friends.

The crew had barely been able to look her or Tai in the eye once it was out. It was like they didn't know what to say. Mila didn't, either. Then one day Tai challenged the silence with, "Look if y'all want to know what happened, ask one of us because half the stuff being said in the streets is dead-ass wrong." After that things went back to normal. It was like once they didn't have to avoid it, nobody talked about it. And if anybody ever asked for details, they must have asked Tai.

Mila was fine with that. All she knew was that Mr. Bryant could get up to a year in jail and would have to put his name on a list of offenders. Whether or not he went to jail, he wasn't allowed anywhere near Mila and couldn't go near center court, the playground, or the rec center where kids hung out. He couldn't even move back home.

Still, some days it was too much. Her dad's constant checking, asking if she was "okay." The bad dreams about Mr. Bryant's hand coming toward her. Her heart feeling so heavy it felt like it was full of rocks. Ms. Sophia looking sad. Feeling like the whole neighborhood was talking about it. Those were the bad days.

But there were fewer of them once school started. And she was going to a counselor.

First, the thought of talking about it over and over, to a stranger, horrified her. But Mila liked the once-a-week sessions now. Rebecca never forced her to talk about anything she didn't want. A few times they'd spent the entire hour talking about dance classes.

Every now and then she still felt like looking over her shoulder when she was outside alone. She also had her doubts that Mr. Bryant would stay away from Ms. Sophia's house forever. But at least, for now, things were as close to normal as they had been in a long time. It's why she had chosen to stay and do TAG. Because for everything she hated about the

Cove, there were some things she loved.

What she loved most was her family. She missed Cinny. But she felt safest at home with her dad and brothers. And now Chrissy and some of the girls in her TAG classes were starting to feel like family.

The Cove was where she belonged.

EPILOGUE—
TAI'S NOVEMBER

Tai loved the mornings. It was the only time the entire squad was together. Whatever they hadn't caught up on the night before, on FriendMe or in a chat, they did at the bus stop.

She almost hated to see the bus come, because once they got to school they had to go their separate ways. And three afternoons a week, everybody but her and Simp left school early to attend their TAG class.

So mornings were her favorite.

Every morning they stood, circled in the same order, talking. Mila, Tai, Rollie, Simp, Sheeda, Mo, Chris, and Chrissy. They were so close that their book bags sometimes bumped each other if they shifted too fast.

The circle was tighter than usual that morning. Partly to keep the wind from whipping in their faces but, Tai couldn't lie, partly to freeze out the handful of sixth and seventh graders standing at the bus stop with them. Every now and then one or two would slink closer, but far enough to keep Tai from gritting on them. They knew better than to join in without being invited.

It was ignorant but that's how it was. Had always been. Eighth graders ruled at the bus stop. Their conversations were the loudest and their circle the biggest as they took up more space than they needed to on the sidewalk.

Tai glanced over her shoulder at the ones who stood on the far fringes of the circle pretending it didn't matter. They'd be all right, though. They'd end up getting tight a little more each year, just like her squad had. And it wasn't nothing like having a squad.

Tai hadn't understood that at first. She had been so used to wanting Bean to herself, she hadn't seen how much the others meant to her. She understood now because they had been there when things blew up.

After Mr. Jamal pressed charges, Tai knew the whole

hood would be squawking about it. She wasn't ready for it, but she didn't let on. Every time she stepped outside she expected to hear the words "Chester the molester" slip out of somebody's mouth. That's who her father was now, to the hood. At least that's what people would think he was. Tai had to act like none of it bothered her because Nona's message was clear—words can't hurt you, we know the truth, don't let people who don't have nothing better to do than gossip get in your head.

They did know the truth—he had touched Bean—and that's what messed with Tai. She didn't know if it was worse that he had touched her, or that he did it because he was high. She knew better than to point that out to Nona, though. Nona said the drugs made him sick. Getting him "better," off the drugs, was all she'd focus on.

So Tai had swallowed the fear making her heart feel like it was running on high speed all day and pretended it didn't matter. She had braced herself for somebody in the squad—Simp most likely, since he never knew what not to say—to ask her what had happened. She was used to people in the Cove being boldly nosy.

But no one had. Not the first day. Or the second. After a while Tai started to wonder if they heard. But it was impossible not to know.

Nona had made her father turn himself in after the charges were filed and when she posted bail for him, she made him go to some rehab way out in the boons. No more dipping in to stay at Nona's a few weeks here and there. He was gone.

So people knew.

Once at the playground, Neesha had made a loud comment about how Tai's father was gonna miss the block party since he couldn't come near the rec. The group she was with had laughed. Before Tai could say something, Mo had loud-mumbled how Neesha was irky and Sheeda had even mustered a loud "Neesha, you wrong," in her direction.

Then Rollie had gone even further, calling Neesha out with, "Ay yo, Neesha, heard your pops up for parole for that drug bid. Good luck on it, for real." It shut Neesha up and the beef had ended there. And she knew then how much she needed her friends. Even Chrissy.

It wasn't that they were tight or anything, but she didn't hate her. Even if she did, there was no getting rid of her. Her and Chris had become part of the group so easily, Tai wasn't even sure when she'd started to semi-get along with the girl.

Having the squad made the whole mess with her father bearable. It was good not having him in the house anymore. The only problem was, some days Nona seemed far away and now Tai knew those were the times she'd gotten a text or call from him, usually with him still pleading his innocence and acting like Nona could spring him from rehab like it was jail.

It still amazed Tai that he didn't get it. He only wasn't in jail because Nona had gotten him a lawyer who told him if he made good on staying clean, the judge would probably fine him and give him probation.

Tai honestly couldn't remember the last time she'd seen her father clean. One night she'd lain in bed trying and not even a single memory slipped in. It made her bawl. She tried imagining how different things would be if he wasn't on drugs, but every image that played in her head looked like a scene from a television show. Fake. Fantasy.

She doubted he'd ever get his self together. Thinking about it was a waste of time. She wished her grandmother would see that.

When Nona went to see him in the rehab, Tai refused to go. Nona never forced it.

The only time she didn't think about him at all was when she was dancing. When the groove hit, the music whipped her body whatever way it wanted and her brain left the building.

It was her first year taking hip-hop officially, but after only two weeks Mr. Sommers had moved her up to H3's Intermediate 2 class.

I2s got to travel. Her first performance with them was in a few weeks, in Virginia. Just thinking about it made Tai's limbs tremble with happiness. With all that went down, she didn't know she could feel happy anymore. Sometimes it felt wrong that she could be happy, knowing how sad Nona was. She tried not to let her thoughts go there.

Right now, with the squad around her, she was happy. She wasn't going to apologize for it.

Suddenly Chris's voice rang out into a song. A few notes in, Rollie rapped under the melody. The two of them vibed off each other all the time, bursting into song or rap anytime it hit them. The loud talking slowed down, then stopped, as everybody listened. The circle closed in a little more, like they were trying to keep the song to themselves.

Sheeda swayed along, eyes closed like it was her

all-time jam. Mo's foot tapped. Bean was watching, a smile on her face.

The song floated in the air: "When I'm with you it's all I can do—to keep my cool and just roll on through. . . . "

Did Rollie know that's exactly how she felt about him? They still weren't exclusive yet, but they sat together on the bus every morning. He texted her outside the group chat all the time. So soon. Very soon.

She smiled at the thought and let the circle's energy wrap around her until she felt as high as she did in dance class.

Above the pettiness.

Above hurt feelings.

Above loneliness.

Above it all.